BUXTON ROOTS

LeeAnn Dickey
with
LeAnn Lemberger
Michael W. Lemberger

PBL Limited
Ottumwa, Iowa

Buxton Roots

This edition published January 2009

10 9 8 7 6 5 4 3 2 1

ISBN 1-892689-72-3

ISBN 13: 978-1-892689-72-6

Illustrations: Pages 5, 90-91, 104: LeeAnn Dickey Collection, used with permission. Pages 3, 6, 7, 8-9: David Longdo Collection, used with permission. Pages 71, 105, 107, 108, 110, 111, 112, 113, 114, 115, 116, 117, 119, 121, 123, 125, 126, 133, 134, 135, 136: Michael W. Lemberger, used with permission. Pages 3, 4, 10, 11, 12, 13, 14, 15, 25, 37, 57, 73, 75, 82, 98: Monroe County Historical Museum Collection, used with permission. Pages 130-131: Lemberger Collection, used with permission.

We wish to acknowledge the assistance of The Monroe County Historical Society, the Women's Archives of the University of Iowa Libraries, and the State Historical Society of Iowa (Iowa City branch), in the research for this book.

Printed in the United States of America

Rights Editor
PBL Limited
P.O. Box 935
Ottumwa IA 52501-0935
pbl@pbllimited.com

Copies of this book are available from PBL Limited. See page 138 for details on ordering by mail, or visit our website at www.pbllimited.com for more information.

Buxton houses. (Longdo collection.)

This book is dedicated to the memory of the people of Buxton and Muchakinock

Dirt street and rail line in the suburb of Coopertown. (Monroe County Historical Museum.)

A Word from the Author

People often ask why I have this fascination with Buxton. While I was researching my own family records, I started volunteering at the Monroe County Genealogical Society library, and I began transcribing records and looking up information for other families, including some -- like the Reasby family -- who had roots in Buxton. That led me to the courthouse records.

It seemed to me that most of the available records concerned the white residents of Buxton. There was seldom a mention of the African-American residents. I was really mad that no one had taken the time to look at the African-American records – because if it wasn't for them, there wouldn't be a story about Buxton. So I decided to compile my own lists.

The records included in this book are the result of more than two years of full-time research.

In the meantime, I became involved in the Pioneer Cemetery Commission. One of the projects we undertook was to clear the Buxton Cemetery, which had been left to grow over in brush. I believe no one should be forgotten.

I haven't included a listing of births, because in that era there was no state requirement to report them, so very few birth records were actually filed at the time of the birth. The listing of marriage records was complied from Marriage Indexes on file at the Monroe County Courthouse. The 1910 census data was assembled from federal census records.

Reasby lunch car, in front of the YMCA. (Monroe County Historical Museum.)

Unknown residents of Buxton. (Dickey collection.)

The book includes two separate listings of deceased residents of Buxton -- a list of death records and a list of known burials in the Buxton cemetery. Information differs somewhat between the two lists. The cemetery listing includes information from stones and from the files of funeral homes. The listing of death records was compiled from the Death Record Index at the Monroe County Courthouse, and often includes more personal information such as parents and place of birth.

The 1935 pension records were originally collected because of a special state census done for the Old Age Pension fund. Every Iowan over the age of 21 was subject to a $2.00 tax which was put into a pension fund for older citizens. Though the tax was discontinued in 1936, the record of this census remains a valuable resource for genealogists. The census is especially important for this book because it lists the only black residents still living in Monroe County at the time. The pension record list was first compiled and transcribed by Rosalie Dicks, a Monroe County Historical Society member.

I wish to thank: My husband and family for helping with the cemetery and for the support they have given me. My dad, John Simmers, for locating research for me. Grace Bloodsworth and Hattie

Chicago and Northwestern Railway, Buxton Depot. (Longdo collection.)

Bloodsworth for getting me started in genealogy. Jeff and Pam Howard for their support in all my research. Tracy Casady and Kim Wynn for their help at the courthouse. Kim Carr-Irvin and Janice Dixon for getting me started in the African-American research in Monroe County and for becoming my good friends. The Mahaska County and Monroe County Genealogical Societies for their work in compiling lists that helped in my research. Floyd Hols, Amanda McGrath, Jim and Rosalie Mullinix, and Merle Regenold for the endless work to restore the Buxton Cemetery, along with the Monroe County Pioneer Cemetery Commission.

Over the years, there have been several books about Buxton. BUXTON ROOTS is intended to be a reference guide to help in the search for families. Is the proof of marriage, death, parents, place of birth available for them to access? Is their lost relative buried in the Buxton cemetery? I hope this book will answer some of their questions and find their missing relatives, by preserving all this important documentation in one easy-to-access place.

I hope you will find the Buxton records both interesting and useful!

--LeeAnn Dickey

Table of Contents

Buxton house. (Longdo collection.)

(above and right) A panoramic view of Buxton, before 1910. (Longdo collection.)

The Buxton Legacy

"Utopia"

Less than 50 years after the Civil War, and just about 50 years before the Civil Rights act, the small, unincorporated town of Buxton, Iowa became a model community where racial integration and equal pay for equal work were the accepted policy, and interracial marriages were not only condoned but celebrated.

In a state where 99 percent of the population at the time was white, the majority of Buxton's population was black. In 1905, 54 percent of the nearly 5,000 residents of Buxton were black.

The largest portion of the black population were coal miners and their families. The workers had been recruited from the South by Consolidation Coal Company, which owned the surrounding coal mines. But Buxton also included black professionals (doctors, pharmacists, dentists, lawyers) and businessmen (farmers, landlords, shopkeepers, restaurateurs).

Both the white and the black residents were treated by the black doctors; the company's chief surgeon was black. They were advised by the black lawyers and shopped at the black-owned stores. Black and white miners worked side by side. Black and white clerks manned the company store together. Black and white families lived next door to one another. Black and white students shared classes, learning from teachers of both races.

The people of Buxton, especially the black population, spoke of the town as Utopia – a place where they were free of the stifling restrictions of race. Ben Buxton, the superintendent of the coal company which built Buxton and employed the miners, would not tolerate anyone who treated blacks unfairly, and he was known to get rid of white employees who mistreated blacks.

In fact, however, integration was not perfect in Buxton. Though separations were not forced, racial

groups still tended to cluster amongst themselves, both socially and geographically. Blacks and whites held separate dances, attended separate churches, and belonged to separate lodges.

Even though by today's standards it was not utopia, it was certainly what some other residents called it: "A good place to live." For its time, Buxton was unique.

Coal

Coal was big business in Iowa during the late 1800s. Initially it was used mainly to cook and to heat houses, especially in areas where timber was scarce and was reserved for building. Coal seams were found to underlie much of south central Iowa. Some deposits were close enough to the surface to dig from simple strip or pit mines, but others ran much deeper and required shafts to be sunk to reach the coal.

By 1870, coal became even more important as industries grew, requiring reliable power. Soon railroads stretched across the nation's midsection. Coal fired the locomotives, providing power to move merchandise and people. And it made sense to produce coal regionally, cutting shipping costs. Railroads leased land and operated mines which produced coal exclusively for the use of the railroads. Because the railroad needed fuel all year round, not just during the bitter winter heating season, miners who worked for the railroad's mines had consistent employment and higher annual wages than other miners were able to achieve.

Coal Camps

Because coal mining was labor intensive and workers were not able to commute great distances to work, coal companies built *coal camps* – small towns located near the mines to house their workers. A coal camp usually consisted of several hundred small houses, a company store, and a school. Some included churches, pool halls, or taverns. In most cases, workers could shop only at the company store. Credit was available to them there, but the monopoly sometimes led to inflated prices.

Most coal camps were intended to be used for no more than a decade. When a group of mines was exhausted, the camp would be moved to a location closer to the new mines which were opening up.

Because of the short anticipated lifespan of the towns, sometimes little attention was paid to aesthetics or even to health concerns such as proper drainage.

One such coal camp, located in Mahaska County about halfway between present-day Oskaloosa and Eddyville, Iowa, was called Muchakinock. Organized in the 1860s, Muchakinock became the first place in Iowa where large numbers of black miners were employed; they were recruited from the South after a labor strike in 1881.

The Chicago & Northwestern Railroad bought out the original owners of the mines around Muchakinock, and the Consolidation Coal Company began producing coal exclusively for the railroad. By 1900 the mines around Muchakinock (sometimes called Muchy) were playing out. The company purchased 8,600 acres of land further south, in Bluff Creek Township, Monroe County, where coal had been discovered. They began to plan new mines and a new town, to be named Buxton in honor of J. E. Buxton, the superintendent of the Consolidation Coal Company at the time. The residents of Muchakinock, once a town of 3,000, would move to the new site, along with their houses and even their churches.

But the new town was to be much bigger and much grander.

Buxton

J.E. Buxton soon retired, and his son Ben became the new superintendent of Consolidation Coal. As the pet project of 25-year-old Ben Buxton, the town of Buxton was an exception in many ways to the coal camps which had preceded it.

Ben Buxton
(Monroe County Historical Museum.)

Consolidation hired an architect, Frank Wetherell, to draw the plans for the new homes, churches, and schools which would be added to those brought from Muchakinock. Wetherell also established the general plan of the town. Buxton was carefully laid out, sited on a rolling section of land which provided drainage and air circulation. As a planned community, it included recreational facilities, churches, and schools, but (officially, at least) no taverns or saloons.

Building of the town started in 1900. By 1910, the population was 5,000. Buxton was the largest unincorporated coal mining community in the state. At one time it was also the largest community in Monroe County, with a larger population than the county seat, Albia.

Each family home – there were about 2,000 in all – was a five- or six-room house sited on at least a quarter-acre of land, space which allowed gardening. Many families also raised chickens, or kept a pig or a cow. Each family had a cistern for water storage, with water delivered by the company from deep wells, the creek, and a storage

Company store, center; two YMCA buildings at left. (Monroe County Historical Museum.)

reservoir. Five-room houses had a living room/parlor, dining room and kitchen downstairs, and two bedrooms upstairs. Six-room houses had an additional bedroom on the main floor. Each family had a coal shed and an outhouse in the back yard.

The YMCA built by the company for its workers was said to be the largest in existence in the United States, with as many as 300 members. The three-story YMCA building, along with an annex intended for boys, included space for lodge meetings and an auditorium that would seat 1,000. Among the speakers hosted there was Booker T. Washington, who drew a more-than-capacity crowd.

There were four elementary schools, and within a few years a high school was built. The school superintendent and high school principal were black, as were many teachers. While there was a whites-only private school in town, the public school system was fully integrated.

The company store, the Monroe Mercantile Company, was operated by Consolidation Coal, but residents and workers were not limited to shopping there. Other businesses were not only tolerated but encouraged. The company store was three full stories at first, but was rebuilt on a slightly-smaller scale after a devastating fire in 1910. The store boasted electric lights, electric elevators, and merchandise acquired by buyers who spent all their time in Chicago and New York. A full-time decorator was on staff to arrange window and floor displays. It was said that customers could buy anything from caskets to safety pins at the company store.

YMCA, with boys' annex at left. (Monroe County Historical Museum.)

Buxton had three newspapers (though not all at the same time), a bank, a millinery shop, a municipal band, women's clubs, fraternal lodges, and two baseball teams – one team was integrated, the other all black.

The work

The mines around Buxton were unionized from the beginning. Workers were paid according to a formula based on the amount of coal they mined, and they received equal pay for equal work. Wages were good – the company's payroll averaged $75,000 per month – and if a family included several miners, the family income was above average for the time, leaving room in the budget for niceties and even luxuries.

Each morning three work trains – each composed of 12 to 15 coaches – took the miners out to the work site, returning them to Buxton in the evening.

The mining methods of the day called for "room and pillar" mining, where sections of the coal seam were left undisturbed as "pillars" to support the roof of the mining area, while the sections between were hollowed out – "rooms" – and the coal taken to the surface. Miners were assigned a "room" and worked there, often with a partner or buddy, until that section of the mine was exhausted. They then received another assignment from the foreman and began excavating a new "room."

Coal was hauled through the mine by mules; some mines were so huge that mules were stabled underground and never returned to the surface. Once at the base of the shaft, the coal cars were lifted by enormous hoists to the surface.

Mining was dangerous, with accidents – and fatalities – occurring on a regular basis. However, Iowa miners did not have to contend with explosive gases, as they did elsewhere, which made the work marginally safer.

The end of Buxton

Coal production in Iowa peaked in 1918 at 9.3 million tons. Because of the heavy demand for coal during World War I, production was stepped up at some of the Buxton mines, and therefore the mines were worked out years earlier than had been projected. By about 1920, Consolidation was mining further from Buxton, creating a longer commute. Eventually the miners, too, moved on. Some followed Consolidation's mining operations, while others moved to Des Moines, Waterloo and Cedar Rapids.

Some of Buxton's buildings were moved to the new locations of Haydock, Consol, and Bucknell. Other buildings, such as the Swedish Lutheran Church, remained in Buxton (the building was destroyed by fire in 1954). Remaining houses were sold for $50 each and moved by their new owners.

The new towns – those established after Buxton – did not operate as coal camps for long. The coal mining industry was beginning to shift to surface mining operations. By 1920, railroads began buying

A rare view inside the company store. (Monroe County Historical Museum.)

coal from other locations, and additional energy sources such as electricity and natural gas became available for heating and cooking. Later yet, coal was superceded by diesel as the fuel of choice for locomotives, and the remaining coal mines in Monroe County were idled.

Consolidation's Mine #19 was closed down after a labor strike, leaving a train of loaded coal cars at the bottom of the shaft, waiting only to be hoisted to the surface.

The legacy of Buxton

After the town of Buxton was disbanded, annual reunions were held for many years. Former Buxton residents would gather near the town site each summer. Former Buxtonites living in Des Moines formed the Buxton Club and even developed a museum there.

The town site of Buxton was entered in the National Register of Historic Places on October 15, 1966. Buxton houses are still extant in the area, and many are still identifiable.

But the real legacy of Buxton lies in the memory of racial integration and harmony. We look back now, from the perspective of an additional 50 years since the Civil Rights act, and are intrigued and amazed by the lessons of Buxton – where blacks and whites lived in harmony.

--LeAnn Lemberger

Train near one of the mine shafts. (Monroe County Historical Museum.)

The first company store. The building burned in 1911. (Monroe County Historical Museum.)

The second company store, built shortly after the fire. (Monroe County Historical Museum.)

Buxton, Iowa was located in Bluff Creek Township, Monroe County, Iowa, directly south of the Mahaska County line and just about midway between the cities of Albia and Oskaloosa. The plat map below shows the names of some of the local landowners. Miami was also the site of coal mines operated by Consolidated Coal Company.

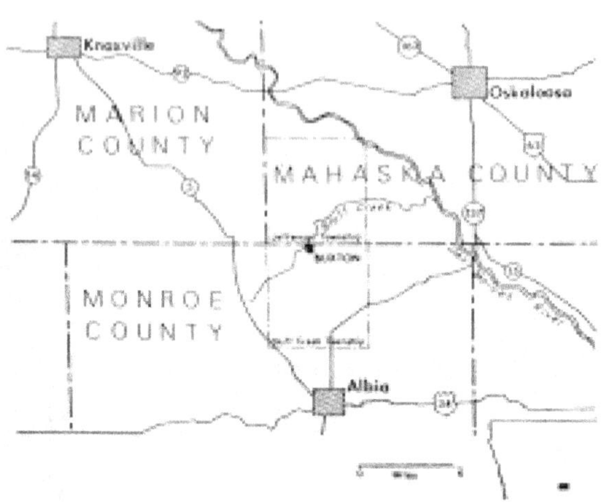

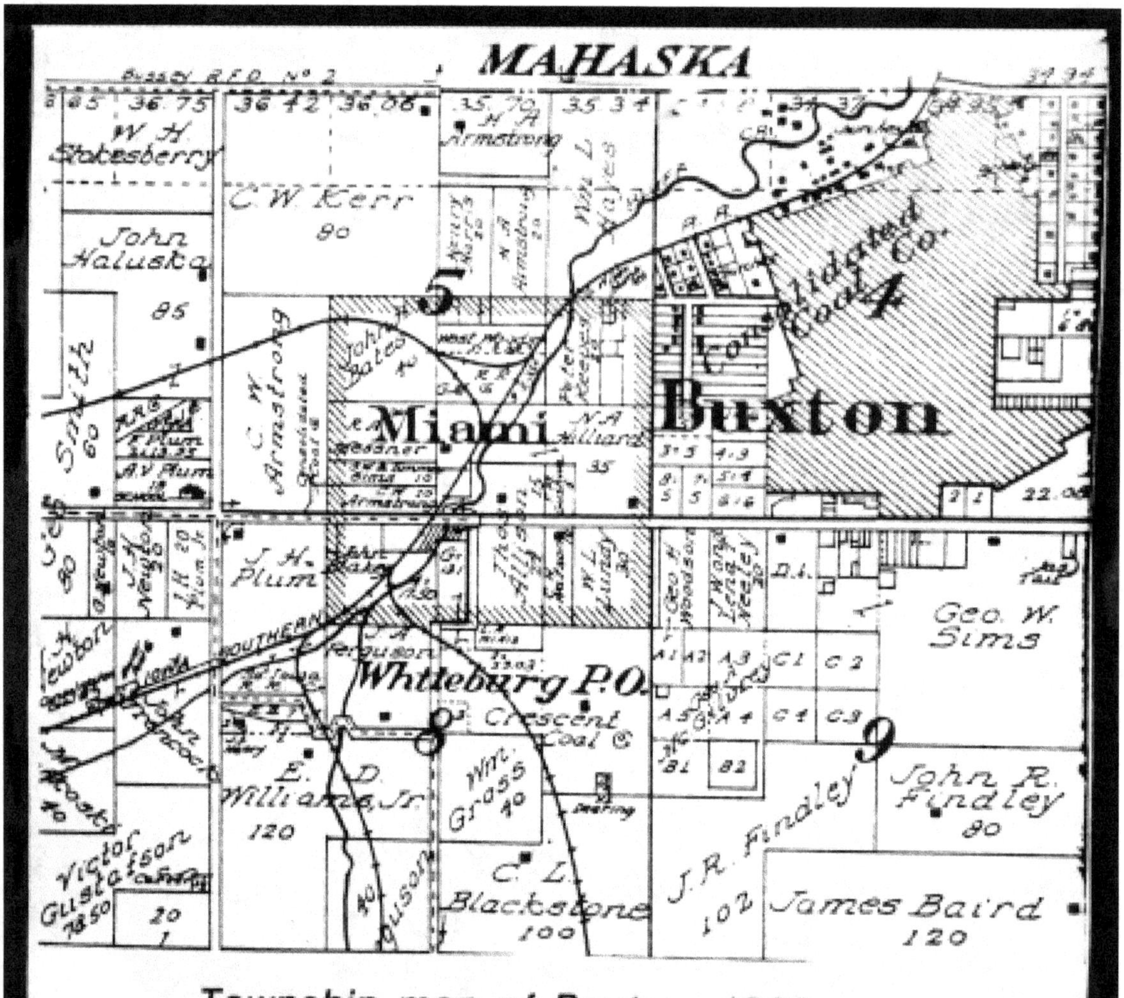

Township map of Buxton, 1900

LeeAnn Dickey

African-American Marriages of Monroe County Iowa

Names are transcribed directly from the county marriage records and are spelled as listed there. A bold **W** denotes a white person. A bold **OB** denotes Old Marriage Record Book.

Groom's name	*Bride's name (maiden)*	Marriage date	**Record Book** Page
Adams, Henry.	*Wells, Lucy.*	February 2, 1904.	**11,** 373
Adams, Monroe.	*Rivers, Maggie (Gray).*	June 1, 1913.	**15,** 519
Alexander, Pete.	*Payne, Mattie B. (Rouse).*	June 4, 1920.	**18,** 189
Allen, Albert.	*Jackson, Dozzie Ester.*	September 28, 1903.	**11,** 250
Allen, Bert.	*Crane, Louisa Ellen.* **W**	April 3, 1923.	**19,** 186
Allen, Charles.	*Barnes, Aggie (Pitts).*	August 29, 1905.	**12,** 251
Allen, Hobart.	*Jones, Sarah.*	September 26, 1925.	**20,** 68
Allen, Jesse C.	*Diggs, Hettie.*	January 1, 1910.	**14,** 224
Allen, John H.	*Arthur, Myrtle.*	September 11, 1918.	**17,** 436
Allen, Philip.	*Smith, Hattie.*	June 8, 1907.	**13,** 153
Allen, William.	*Hawkins, Rachel (Hockings).*	January 31, 1906.	**12,** 383
Allen, William B.	*Glenn, Mattie.*	December 27, 1905.	**12,** 356
Ampey, Carl.	*Darden, Willie Belle.*	April 3, 1916.	**16,** 561
Anderson, Fred.	*Godetts, Doris.*	March 16, 1916.	**16,** 552
Anderson, James Taylor	*Lewis, Ora Louise.*	June 17, 1914.	**16,** 163
Anderson, John W.	*Garnett, Ruth A.*	November 8, 1909.	**14,** 175
Arbuckle, Jerry H.	*Garland, Julia A. (Reasby).*	December 9, 1905.	**12,** 336
Atkinson, Milton.	*Henley, Lulu.*	October 26, 1910.	**14,** 428
Austin, Winzer.	*Curtis, Lulu (Weir-Terry).*	October 27, 1904.	**12,** 7
Baker, George.	*Washington, Daisy.*	November 7, 1903.	**11,** 291
Baker, John.	*Fields, Minnie.* **W**	November 12, 1906.	**13,** 25
Baker, John A.	*Cannon, Mary (McKinney).*	July 1, 1908.	**13,** 400
Baker, John A.	*Qualls, Sadie M.*	January 31, 1918.	**11,** 317
Baker, Paul F.	*Garnett, Lizzie.*	January 19, 1918.	**17,** 314
Baldin, N.J. **W**	*Davis, Lela (Dixtson).*	July 3, 1919.	**17,** 586
Ball, Lloyd Leonard.	*Vandevier, Opal Mae.*	October 30, 1923.	**19,** 330
Ballard, C.C.	*Neal, Lulu (Jackson).*	March 15, 1904.	**11,** 401
Barber, Charles.	*Burton, Mary.* **W**	April 24, 1920.	**18,** 161
Barber, Rice.	*Welch, Winnie (Allen).*	September 27, 1904.	**11,** 552

Groom's name	*Bride's name (maiden)*	Marriage date	**Record Book** Page
Bates, John S.	*Lockett, Lula Belle.*	November 12, 1907.	**13,** 255
Bedford, Lewis.	*McNeal, Sarah A.*	February 21, 1910.	**14**, 265
Bell, Emmett.	*Lewis, Thelma.*	February 17, 1920.	**18**, 108
Bennett, Asa.	*Carey, Lucinda.*	November 30, 1908.	**13,** 501
Benning, Walter A.	*Grayson, Hattie.*	April 17, 1910.	**14**, 316
Bentley, James.	*Jones, Jennie.* **W**	March 19, 1906.	**12**, 432
Biugham, Warver.	*Dardon, Willabelle.*	March 7, 1921.	**18**, 376
Black, Bailey.	*Cross, Lemmer.*	December 26, 1908.	**13,** 522
Blackman, Early.	*Reeves, Fannie (Brown).*	November 8, 1913.	**15**, 635
Blaine, William.	*Cato, Rachel.*	March 4, 1923.	**19,** 170
Blakey, Andrew.	*Stepp, Vetta.*	November 3, 1903.	**11,** 285
Blakey, Frank.	*Doyle, Leatha.*	December 13, 1911.	**15,** 148
Blaney, John W.	*Watkins, Lizzie.*	July 2, 1916.	**16**, 614
Blue, Robert.	*Scott, Iva (Tyrrell).*	June 29, 1921.	**18**, 458
Bolden, Mat.	*Fuqua, Rosa (Baldwin).*	June 11, 1913.	**15**, 535
Bolden, Philip H.	*Spears, Ora E.*	May 14, 1910.	**14,** 332
Bolden, Sterling.	*Taylor, Flora.*	June 18, 1902.	**OB 10,** 31
Bolden, Sterling C.	*Bradshaw, Agnes.*	December 7, 1905.	**12,** 338
Boles, Henry.	*Fairfax, Ella L. (Baker).*	September 28, 1907.	**13,** 220
Boles, Henry.	*Tansel, Minnie May.*	December 26, 1916.	**17,** 84
Boles, Henry Jr.	*Watson, Essie May.*	May 28, 1913.	**15**, 521
Boles, Robert.	*Lowery, Elsie Geneva.*	February 19, 1913.	**15**, 445
Bond, James.	*Nicholson, Cleo.*	April 16, 1901.	**OB 10,**12
Booker, Henry.	*Clay, Lottie May.*	June 13, 1905.	**12,** 198
Boston, Clarence.	*Walker, Alice.*	September 10, 1910.	**14,** 401
Boston, Clarence Walter.	*Garland, Bessie Ann.*	February 18, 1926.	**20,** 125
Bowers, Walter.	*Brown, Minnie.*	February 23, 1927.	**20,** 283
Bowlin, Essa W.	*Payne, Calla L.*	May 12, 1904.	**11**, 451
Bowman, George W.	*Bryson, Pearl (Garland).*	June 1, 1914.	**16,** 150
Bradshaw, Joseph.	*Johnson, Gertrude (Mays).*	April 18, 1909.	**14**, 24
Brewer, Jonathan.	*Meadows, Josie.*	October 29, 1903.	**11,** 279
Briggs, George.	*Watkins, Mollie (Jackson).*	February 21, 1911.	**14,** 528
Brinker, Charles.	*Saunders, Sarita.*	April 18, 1911.	**14**, 563
Bronson, Samuel.	*Patrick, Agnes.*	September 27, 1920.	**18,** 273
Brookins, Andrew Jackson.	*Walker, Eva.*	May 12, 1910.	**14,** 330
Brooks, James E.	*Carter, Kate.*	January 28, 1914.	**16,** 53
Brooks, Leonard.	*Garrett, Florence.*	September 30, 1922.	**19,** 64
Brooks, William J.	*Graham, Luella.*	February 12, 1907.	**13,** 90

LeeAnn Dickey

Groom's name	*Bride's name (maiden)*	Marriage date	**Record Book** Page
Brookwell, Andrew F.	*Oliphant, Carrie.*	March 3, 1904.	**11,** 395
Brown, Earl E.	*Lobbins, Pansy M.*	March 27, 1916.	**16,** 558
Brown, Ellis E.	*Fletcher, Julia.*	January 14, 1908.	**13,** 290
Brown, George.	*Duncan, Gertrude.*	July 30, 1906.	**12,** 510
Brown, George.	*Stewart, Myrtle (Luckett).*	December 7, 1915.	**16,** 480
Brown, George.	*Harris, Mattie Elizabeth (Dival).*	March 30, 1918.	**11,** 344
Brown, Grant.	*Jewitt, Kate Mrs.*	May 14, 1903.	**11,** 166
Brown, Grant.	*Carey, Alice (Walker).*	September 11, 1912.	**15,** 311
Brown, Grant.	*Robinson, Pearl (Sawyer).*	February 23, 1923.	**19,** 160
Brown, Jacob Jr.	*Jones, Katheryn.*	February 11, 1922.	**18,** 596
Brown, Marshall.	*Abington, Lulu (Ball/Bell).*	November 24, 1904.	**12,** 22
Brown, Raymond.	*Burkett, Ruth.*	April 27, 1926.	**20,** 156
Brown, Robert W.	*Richey, Estella.*	December 24, 1923.	**19,** 371
Brown, S. Joe.	*Wilson, Sue.*	December 31, 1902.	**11,** 64
Brown, Velton.	*Beaman, Beatrice.*	October 6, 1923.	**19,** 307
Brown, William.	*Benning, Burnettie.*	April 11, 1901.	**OB 10,** 12
Bryant, Lawrence.	*Cary, Cleopatra.*	November 25, 1916.	**17,** 71
Bryant, Orville.	*Robison, Mamie.*	March 3, 1910.	**14,** 275
Bryant, Otho.	*Harriett, Nellie.*	February 19, 1906.	**12,** 403
Bryson, James/Eugene.	*Stewart, Esther May.*	July 30, 1923.	**19,** 260
Bryson, Jeff.	*Brown, Pearl.*	January 11, 1925.	**19,** 565
Bryson, William S.	*Davis, Sarah M. (Lay)*	February 19, 1912.	**15,** 203
Buford, Elmer.	*Bowers, Joanna.*	September 12, 1927.	**20,** 360
Buford, John.	*Priestly, Mary (Irvin).*	November 3. 1903.	**11,** 284
Buford, John.	*Niles, Minnie.*	September 28, 1901.	**OB 10,** 18
Burgess, Howard.	*Gillenwaters, Ellen Hunter.*	October 23, 1906.	**13,** 7
Burkett, Henry.	*Jackson, Maggie.*	September 16, 1909.	**14,** 130
Burkett, John.	*Rumley, Leona.*	October 10, 1922.	**19,** 71
Burkett, Robert.	*Carpenter, Susanna.*	May 10, 1911.	**15,** 11
Burks, Herman E.	*Reasby, Vennetta B.*	March 29, 1916.	**16,** 559
Burns, Emory M.	*Edmond, Nancy.*	June 20, 1914.	**16,** 167
Burns, Henry.	*Green, Rosa.*	September 25, 1907.	**13,** 215
Burns, Jessie.	*Bates, Eva Effie.*	June 5, 1907.	**13,** 147
Burton, H.C.	*Taylor, Oleva.*	September 18, 1920.	**18,** 266
Burton, James A.	*Howard, Fannie.*	October 20, 1905.	**12,** 287
Burton, Westley.	*Williams, Pauline.*	February 7, 1920.	**18,** 97
Buttram, George.	*Graves, Bell (King).*	February 26, 1917.	**17,** 123

Groom's name	*Bride's name (maiden)*	Marriage date	**Record Book** Page
Byers, Lloyd.	*Phillips, Lucile.*	November 10, 1909.	**14**, 180
Campbell, George H.	*Wilson, Nannie.*	November 10, 1902.	**11**, 26
Campbell, Henry Y.	*Jefferson, Abbie.*	July 28, 1903.	**11**, 208
Cannady, Robert C.	*Gunn, Aline.*	February 29, 1912.	**15**, 208
Carey, E.C.	*Freeman, Mary.*	January 26, 1921.	**18**, 353
Carey, Peter F.	*Blaney, Mary F. Mrs.*	November 2, 1909.	**14**, 167
Carey, Robert.	*Jones, Bessie.*	April 13, 1904.	**11**, 430
Carey, Robert.	*Taylor, Lee Oney.*	June 22, 1910.	**14**, 358
Carpenter, Archie.	*Junkins, Mable.*	April 1, 1918.	**17**, 346
Carpenter, Archie.	*Walker, Hazel.*	December 31, 1926.	**20**, 268
Carpenter, Arthur.	*Shade, Ella (Jars).*	August 16, 1911.	**15**, 67
Carr, Earnest.	*Humbles, Stella.*	April 27, 1917.	**17**, 158
Carr, George.	*Robinson, Mary F.*	March 23, 1912.	**15**, 219
Carter, Clinton.	*Parkey, Ida M.*	November 25, 1915.	**16**, 477
Carter, Edward Albert.	*Warren, Rose Etta.*	June 13, 1908.	**13**, 396
Carter, Edward L.	*Mardis, Pearl E.*	December 25, 1912.	**15**, 391
Carter, Henry.	*Ewing, Iuice.*	October 26, 1921.	**18**, 528
Carter, James.	*Edgar, Leenetta.*	August 23, 1915.	**16**, 425
Carter, Otto.	*Branch, Eva.*	June 7, 1907.	**13**, 152
Carter, William.	*Ewing, Octavia.*	November 4, 1910.	**14**, 433
Carter, William.	*Stokes, Rosa (Turner).*	April 18, 1917.	**17**, 150
Carter, William Lawrence.	*Clark, Danelee.*	August 1, 1917.	**17**, 213
Cary, Aaron.	*Johnson, Emma.*	September 24, 1904.	**11**, 550
Cavil, Charles.	*Holland, Isabella.*	November 21, 1904.	**12**, 17
Cavil, Charles Dewey.	*Weaver, Willie Lewis.*	July 9, 1919.	**17**, 589
Chambers, James.	*Fields, Cora.*	February 7, 1905.	**12**, 101
Cheatham, Garnett.	*Cross, Vetta.*	July 12, 1916.	**16**, 624
Chocklette, Wm.	*Patterson, Mary (Wadlington).*	November 2, 1918.	**17**, 462
Clark, Joseph.	*Johnson, Orvil.*	December 9, 1901.	**OB 10**, 22
Clay, Henry.	*Wilson, Mary (Oliphant).*	March 11, 1907.	**13**, 103
Claybrooke, Andrew J.	*Hartwell, Annie Eliza.*	December 15, 1904.	**12**, 60
Claybrooke, Richard.	*London, Hattie B.*	June 6, 1906.	**12**, 476
Clayburn, Harry.	*Jackson, Mary.*	September 27, 1920.	**18**, 275
Clements, John Willie.	*Jones, Roberta.*	November 29, 1926.	**20**, 252
Coleman, Allen G.	*Wilson, Ione.*	December 31, 1925.	**20**, 109
Coleman, Fred.	*Wilson, Lorna.*	October 15, 1918.	**17**, 456
Coleman, Fred E.	*Washington, Willa A. (Perkins).*	December 14, 1910.	**14**, 464

Groom's name	*Bride's name (maiden)*	Marriage date	**Record Book** Page
Coleman, Thornton A.	*Poindexter, Anna (Black).*	November 20, 1907.	**13**, 260
Coles, Daniel T.	*Massey, Alice.*	December 2, 1903.	**11**, 321
Collier, Hicks.	*Clay, Bessie (Wright).*	October 23, 1916.	**17**, 46
Collins, David.	*Huston, Sarah A.* **W**	January 25, 1904.	**11**, 367
Con, James.	*Rumley, Levice.*	June 21, 1924.	**19**, 457
Cook, James L.	*Beaman, Lizzie.*	July 5, 1904.	**11**, 488
Cooper, Charles.	*Wheels, Jennie.*	August 16, 1910.	**14**, 385
Cooper, Ed. **W**	*Lewis, Priscilla.*	March 10, 1923.	**19**, 176
Cornish, Isaiah.	*Hagens, Clara.*	May 8, 1905.	**12**, 175
Cowser, Shepherd D.	*Coleman, Margaret M.*	December 8, 1904.	**12**, 52
Cozart, Joseph.	*Wright, Julia.*	October 10, 1905.	**12**, 274
Craddock, Lee V.	*Green, Annie.*	September 25, 1905.	**12**, 260
Crayton, Fred.	*Wiseman, Laura.*	November 27, 1903.	**11**, 314
Cropp, Delois.	*Burke, Margaret.*	November 7, 1922.	**19**, 94.
Cross, William C.	*Lewis, Maggie.*	October 2, 1909.	**14**, 147
Crowley, Ralph T.	*Mundon, Mary Mrs. (Watts).* **W**	November 9, 1907.	**13**, 252
Dabney, Charles E.	*Cobbs, Hallie.*	April 20, 1910.	**14**, 317
Dammons, James M.	*Holmes, Mary L. (Darry).*	August 8, 1904.	**11**, 508
Dammons, Jasper M.	*Wright, Mary (Snead).*	December 9, 1915.	**16**, 482
Daniels, H.D.	*Watkins, Florence.*	May 3, 1921.	**18**, 412
Daniels, William.	*Stone, Icy (Brent).*	September 20, 1904.	**11**, 543
Darden, William.	*Blocker, Mary (Holenbeck).*	May 29, 1907.	**13**, 146
Davis, B.L.	*McMath, Rosa (Davis).*	May 20, 1922.	**19**, 5
Davis, Eugene.	*Tate, Zelma.*	May 11, 1921.	**18**, 418
Davis, George W.	*Taylor, Dora.*	November 2, 1906.	**12**, 530
Davis, Isiah.	*Harris, Alberta.*	January 8, 1926.	**20**, 112
Davis, John H.	*Page, Edith M.*	November 16, 1904.	**12**, 14
Deal, William.	*Garland, Emma V. (Fields).* **W**	April 22, 1911.	**14**, 566
Deering, Handy.	*Simons, Mammie.*	August 19, 1910.	**14**, 387
Demley Wilmore E.	*Oliver, Lillie.*	August 24, 1908.	**13**, 432
Devorst, Lee.	*Jackson, Mamie Etta.*	April 8, 1907.	**13**, 123
Dibrell, Ernest.	*Moore, Addie.*	December 15, 1923.	**19**, 357
Dixon, Tyler.	*Robinson, Mattie.*	May 26, 1904.	**11**, 461
Douglass, Frank A.	*Carter, Hattie Bell (Price).*	October 26, 1911.	**15**, 114
Downs, Ed J.	*Wilson, Maggie.*	December 13, 1904.	**12**, 59
Doyle, Peter.	*Carr, Mary Belle.*	January 1, 1903.	**11**, 67
Dudley, Lewis.	*Edmonds, Anna Belle.*	April 24, 1920.	**18**, 158

Groom's name	*Bride's name (maiden)*	Marriage date	**Record Book** Page
Dupree, William L.	*King, Nannie (Brown).*	July 24, 1906.	**12**, 504
Dysart, Fred.	*Buchanan, Mabel.*	January 23, 1905.	**12**, 83
Eaves, Arthur W.	*Boston, Alice L. (Walker).*	May 6, 1916.	**16**, 581
Eaves, Charles H.	*Payne, Ethel.*	October 23, 1912.	**15**, 348
Edinbugh, E.	*Walker, Mildora.*	October 11, 1920.	**18**, 283
Edinburgh, E.	*Jackson, Mary.*	January 24, 1925.	**19**, 569
Edmond, Harry.	*Shelton, Thelma.*	September 11, 1922.	**19**, 51
Edmonds, Lus.	*Scott, Mary.*	December 22, 1917.	**17**, 301
Edwards, David.	*Edwards, Grace L. (Darnell).* **W**	March 16, 1911.	**14**, 547
Edwards, Leff.	*Carthan, Sarah.*	December 9, 1901.	**OB 10**, 22
Elliott, Charles Otis.	*Logan, Rose Alma Viola.*	December 24, 1906.	**13**, 51
Elliott, George Jr.	*Douglas, Gladys.*	November 4, 1921.	**18**, 532
Embra, Charley.	*Warthol, Mary.*	December 29, 1900.	**OB 10**, 8
Estes, Arthur J.	*Grayson, Nellie.*	November 29, 1906.	**13**, 36
Evans, Roy.	*Whisiker, Emma (Wilson).*	July 22, 1916.	**16,** 629
Ewing, Robert Jr.	*Larson, Ethel.*	April 16, 1923.	**19**, 204
Farley, Eldra L.	*Roach, Mary Louise.*	August 1, 1917.	**17**, 212
Farrar, John H.	*Green, Rosa L.*	October 29, 1902.	**11**, 15
Ferguson, Lewis.	*Lindsey, Martha.*	April 21, 1904.	**11,** 434
Finley, Joseph D.	*Poindexter, Mary K.*	December 21, 1905.	**12,** 343
Fisher, Ernest M.	*Sheldon, Galena.*	September 30, 1905.	**12,** 264
Fletcher, Arthur M.	*Wilson, Nannie E.*	November 14, 1911.	**15**, 126
Foster, Chas. L.	*Stevenson, Ruby (Cornelius).*	November 17, 1919.	**18,** 36
Franklin, Forest.	*Howard, Luella.*	January 8, 1927.	**20**, 269
Franklin, Thos. Geo.	*Bickley, Vivian.*	February 14, 1910.	**14**, 259
French, LaFayette.	*Mallette, Lela Nelson.*	March 16, 1905.	**12**, 136
Fry, Charles.	*Murray, Anna (Morrison).*	March 3, 1905.	**12,** 126
Fulwood, William F.	*Hannan, Elizabeth (Jackson).*	October 4, 1913.	**15**, 610
Gaines, Andrew.	*Snoddy, Maidie.*	April 10, 1904.	**11**, 427
Gaines, Moses.	*Brown, Anna A.*	March 12, 1904.	**11,** 403*
Gardner, Ed.	*Davis, Maggie (Gider).*	September 1, 1920.	**18**, 253
Garland, George.	*Robinson, Manie.*	October 21, 1922.	**19**, 81
Garland, Jack.	*Crews, Mamie .*	June 20, 1927.	**20**, 323
Garland, Jackson.	*Garland, Viola M. (Reaver).*	April 8, 1907.	**13**, 120
Garland, John L.	*Dorsey, Pearl.*	August 12, 1914.	**16,** 190
Garland, William H.	*Leek, Mattie.*	November 24, 1907.	**13**, 245
Garland, Wilson.	*Orr, Dixie.*	June 19, 1916.	**16**, 603

Groom's name	*Bride's name (maiden)*	Marriage date	**Record Book** Page
Garnett, James L.	*Carson, Virgie L.*	December 6, 1904.	**12**, 49
Garnett, Westley.	*Brown, Grace.*	February 2, 1918.	**17,** 318
Garnett, William.	*Barnes, Vicey (Robinson).*	November 10, 1920.	**18**, 294
Garrett, Lee G.	*Carter, Hattie B. (Price).*	November 2, 1905.	**12,** 295
Gasland, George E.	*Brooks, Fanny.*	June 16, 1916.	**16**, 604
Gay, Eugene.	*Moppin, Lena B.*	June 12, 1909.	**14**, 61
Gilliam, Charles Wesley.	*Walden, Stella Gertrude.*	April 23, 1907.	**13,** 129
Gillispie, Henry.	*Davis, Jennie.*	August 29, 1904.	**11**, 523
Glover, William.	*Riley, Mrs. Millie (Woodfork).*	January 26, 1922.	**18**, 589
Goldman, Lee.	*Waters, Sadie.*	February 14, 1919.	**17,** 509
Goodall, Herman.	*Jacobs, Ethel.*	July 30, 1921.	**18**, 475
Gordon, Charles.	*Crawford, Emma Lee.*	August 5, 1913.	**15**, 565
Gordon, Charles.	*Graham, Ruby.*	April 11, 1924.	**19,** 412
Gordon, Gus.	*Sims, Ida (Glen).*	April 6, 1918.	**17**, 348
Gordon, Vernice.	*Vaugh, Edith.*	May 17, 1926.	**20**, 163
Grant, John A.	*Diggs, Mary.*	January 23, 1905.	**12,** 92
Graves, Dan.	*Blaine, Rachel (Cato).*	February 17, 1926.	**20**, 124
Graves, James.	*Alexander, Melvin M.*	January 22, 1926.	**20**, 115
Gravitt, Richard.	*Jones, Leona (Findley).*	September 29, 1922.	**19,** 63
Grayson, Roy A.	*Davis, Bessie L.*	December 25, 1907.	**13**, 273
Green, Callis.	*Turner, Rosa.*	November 25, 1904.	**12,** 29
Green, Emery.	*Rhodes, Iva.*	March 22, 1919.	**17**, 527
Grever, Henry Jr.	*Brown, Cornelia.*	December 24, 1902.	**11**, 58
Greviers, Henry.	*Underdew, Hester.*	October 29, 1902.	**11**, 17
Grievous, Henry.	*Watkins, Louisa (Douglass).*	January 13, 1906.	**12**, 375
Griffith, Arthur.	*Palmer, Edith.*	December 12, 1903.	**11**, 330
Griffith, Samuel.	*Dameron, Cora.*	November 27, 1903.	**11**, 315
Guess, John.	*Williams, Georgia (Brown).*	October 29, 1906.	**13,** 11
Gunter, J.W.	*Ross, Arta (Turner).*	March 2, 1922.	**18**, 605
Guy, Alfred.	*Vaugh, Anna (Coles).*	July 23, 1904.	**11,** 495
Guy, Fountain.	*Ampey, Eva.*	March 5, 1903.	**11,** 121
Guy, Harold.	*Thomas, Frances.*	August 3, 1925.	**20**, 39
Hackett, Clarence.	*Price, Elizabeth.*	June 14, 1914.	**16,** 159
Hale, Hays.	*Edmonson, Polly (Wilson).*	June 27, 1904.	**11,** 481
Hale, Hays.	*Trussell, Mary.* **W**	November 29, 1909.	**14**, 197
Hale. Robert.	*Blackburn, Ella (Gordon).*	October 24, 1903.	**11,** 273
Hampton, William.	*Green, Annie (Miner).*	February 26, 1902.	**OB 10,** 26
Harris, Floyd.	*Buford, Gladys.*	November 7, 1926.	**20,** 244

Groom's name	*Bride's name (maiden)*		Marriage date	**Record Book** Page
Harris, George H.	*Freeman, Mary.*		December 8, 1923.	**19**, 356
Harris, John B.	*Gore, Lois.*		October 24, 1900.	**OB 10,** 6
Harris, John W.	*Bryant, Gabrella.*		May 9, 1906.	**12,** 459
Harrold, Jones.	*King, Mary.*		March 28, 1910.	**14**, 298
Harvey, Alex.	*Ward, Louise.*		July 15, 1919.	**17**, 591
Harvey, Daniel.	*Hughes, Addie.*		December 24, 1900.	**OB 10,** 8
Harvey, Irvin.	*McCann, Elizabeth.*		February 28, 1905.	**12**, 122
Harvey, James W.	*Nelson, Binkey.*		September 2, 1903.	**11,** 229
Harvey, Lewis.	*Atkinson, Mary.*		March 1, 1904.	**11**, 391
Harvey, Norman.	*Randolph, Mary.*	**W**	January 31, 1915.	**16**, 302
Hays, John.	*Brown, Eliza.*		January 19, 1905.	**12**, 90
Haywood, Lucian.	*Stepp, Vetta (Reeves).*		May 18, 1902.	**OB 10,** 32
Henderson, Augustus P.	*Hooks, Laura (Williams).*		November 12, 1912.	**15**, 369
Henderson, John H.	*Young, Fannie.*		August 29, 1904.	**11**, 522
Henderson, Nicholas.	*Johnson, Ola.*		November 12, 1908.	**13**, 484
Hill, Charles L.	*Gaines, Laura.*		January 22, 1906.	**12**, 379
Hill, Daniel.	*Farmer, Polly.*		May 11, 1905.	**12**, 179
Hill, Emil.	*Smith, Ollie (Lasater).*		May 10, 1915.	**16**, 367
Hill, Govner.	*Johnson, Mary Louisa.*		October 15, 1908.	**13**, 462
Hoggsett, Sherman.	*Fraidley, Eva.*		April 17, 1909.	**14,** 23
Hogsette, Sherman.	*Turner, Bessie (Jones).*		October 1, 1921.	**18**, 513
Holland, William G.	*Anderson, Cornelia.*		April 13, 1908.	**13,** 345
Hollingsworth, Creola.	*Bowman, Ezzoe Marguerite.*		February 10, 1915.	**16**, 310
Hornburger, Nathan.	*Mathews, Mary E. (Williams).*		June 28, 1911.	**15**, 47
Hornburger, Nathan.	*Reuben, Laura (Thompson).*		January 25, 1927.	**20,** 276
Horne, David O.	*Stewart, Alice (Greaves).*		March 31, 1909.	**14,** 9
Hoskins, Bud.	*Samuels, Mollie.*		May 31, 1904.	**11**, 463
Hubbard, Archie.	*Wesley, Elizabeth.*		September 27, 1913.	**15**, 600
Hubbard, John M.	*Hub, Loretta.*		December 2, 1908.	**13**, 503
Hubbard, Nathaniel.	*Currigan, Julia (Furguson).*		July 11, 1904.	**11**, 491
Hughes, George H.	*Edmonds, Bettie Mrs. (Hamman).*		April 13, 1908.	**13**, 344
Hull, Geo. W.	*Penman, Goldie (Pennel).*		February 12, 1906.	**12**, 395
Humbles, John C.	*Moore, Lena A.*		December 12, 1911.	**15**, 147
Humbles, William.	*Finley, Mayme (Pondexter).*		May 28, 1919.	**17**, 559
Hunt, James C.	*Johnson, Nellie.*		September 2, 1904.	**11**, 514
Hunter, Virgil.	*Thomas, Ethel.*		August 8, 1910.	**14,** 381
Hurt, Abraham B.	*Yates, Alice.*		September 28, 1909.	**14**, 141
Jackson, Elbert.	*Taylor, Ethel.*		October 6, 1923.	**19**, 309

Main Street, looking west toward Mine #14. (Monroe County Historical Museum.)

Winter in Buxton. (Monroe County Historical Museum.)

Groom's name	*Bride's name (maiden)*	Marriage date	**Record Book** Page
Jackson, Geo. W.	*Bolden, Flora (Taylor).*	February 7, 1906.	**12**, 387
Jackson, George W.	*Brown, Mattie J. Mrs. (Jones).*	November 25, 1907.	**13**, 261
Jackson, Harry E.	*Stevens, Anna (Harris).*	July 1, 1913.	**15**, 550
Jackson, Henry W.	*Weston, Lizzie.*	June 12, 1907.	**13**, 157
Jackson, John.	*Clark, Lissie (Jackson).*	August 30, 1904.	**11**, 524
Jackson, Lewis.	*Woodford, Laura.*	November 18, 1909.	**14**, 188
Jackson, Marcus.	*Prentice, Irene.*	February 28, 1920.	**18**, 124
Jackson, Samuel.	*Lewis, Ann (Kenney).*	March 23, 1909.	**14**, 1
Jackson, Sesco.	*Rhodes, Bessie.*	October 17, 1907.	**13**, 232
Jackson, William.	*Williams, Mary (Linzey).*	March 28, 1904.	**11**, 415
Jackson, Wilson J.	*Calloway, Martha (Arnold).*	December 3, 1910.	**14**, 460
James, Burnette Allen.	*Willis/Wilson, Evelyn M.*	September 22, 1909.	**14**, 134
Jefferson, Andrew J.	*Harris, Lola (Gore).*	June 24, 1907.	**13**, 160
Jefferson, George E.	*Washington, Lenna.*	November 25, 1903.	**11**, 304
Jefferson, Jacob.	*Harper, Virginia (Robinson).*	March 20, 1919.	**17**, 526
Jefferson, John.	*Coleman, Birdie (Kyle).*	November 27, 1909.	**14**, 195
Jefferson, John.	*Ousley, Idella (Woods).*	January 7, 1921.	**18**, 324
Jefferson, Thomas.	*Lewis, Fannie.*	November 26, 1913.	**16**, 12
Jefferson, William.	*McMullen, Cyletha.*	December 25, 1913.	**16**, 35
Jefferson, William F.	*Nelson, Sarah A.*	March 16, 1910.	**14**, 286
Jenkins, James.	*Marshall, Lena.*	October 25, 1919.	**18**, 22
Jenkins, John.	*Grundy, Irene (McCoy).*	February 3, 1909.	**13**, 541
Jenkins, Samuel J.	*Wallace, Janie Bell.*	March 11, 1906.	**12**, 417
Jenkins, Samuel J.	*Wilson, Flora Lee.*	July 2, 1913.	**15**, 548
Jenkins, Samuel J.	*Carter, Eugene (Bardpham).*	May 27, 1919.	**17**, 560
Jewett, William.	*Ampy, Margaret.*	January 27, 1915.	**16**, 241
Johnson, A. J.	*Burgess, Frances.*	May 14, 1918.	**17**, 358
Johnson, B. H.	*Buckner, Edna E. (Stafford).*	July 29, 1918.	**17**, 407
Johnson, Clyde.	*Lewis, Ethel.*	April 22, 1922.	**18**, 625
Johnson, Duncan.	*Brant, Mary Elizabeth.*	December 14, 1911.	**15**, 151
Johnson, Elmer.	*McKerson, Myrtle.*	April 23, 1917.	**17**, 154
Johnson, Frank.	*Johnson, Sarah.*	October 5, 1901.	**OB 10**, 19
Johnson, George L.	*Johnson, Mazie.*	March 1, 1920.	**18**, 117
Johnson, Gustan.	*Smith, Fannie J. (Coles).*	April 8, 1905.	**12**, 148
Johnson, Isaac.	*Ballard, Hattie (Head).*	August 13, 1915.	**16**, 417
Johnson, John W.	*Riggs, Mary A.*	September 7, 1904.	**11**, 532
Johnson, Samuel.	*Howard, Rosie.*	June 12, 1900.	**OB 10**, 3
Johnson, William.	*Blackwell, Worthy.*	March 8, 1909.	**13**, 570

Groom's name	*Bride's name (maiden)*	Marriage date	**Record Book** Page
Jones, Adolph.	*Brown, Alice.*	December 12, 1911.	**15**, 149
Jones, Allen.	*Bibb, Minnie May.*	April 6, 1921.	**18**, 393
Jones, Benj. H.	*Franklin, Jessica.*	August 6, 1910.	**14**, 380
Jones, Bennie Jr.	*Edmonds, Dora.*	November 10, 1923.	**19**, 338
Jones, Bert.	*Palmer, Beulah Beatrice.*	May 11, 1922.	**18**, 638
Jones, Booker.	*Howard, Pauline.*	February 26, 1927.	**20**, 284
Jones, Charles P.	*Ellis, Lulu.*	May 9, 1904.	**11**, 448
Jones, Dassless.	*Buford, Reola.*	June 15, 1916.	**16**, 602
Jones, Ed Jr.	*Smith, Gladys.*	June 22, 1922.	**19**, 23
Jones, Fred.	*Hays, Florence.*	October 13, 1914.	**16**, 237
Jones, George.	*Jackson, Ida.*	March 8, 1921.	**18**, 377
Jones, James.	*Coleman, Hattie.*	November 26, 1906.	**13**, 33
Jones, Joe.	*Smith, May.*	April 24, 1926.	**20**, 154
Jones, John J.	*Ball, Sarah E.*	August 16, 1923.	**19**, 268
Jones, Joseph C.	*Cox, Lellie M.*	August 11, 1903.	**11**, 213
Jones, Robert H.	*Walker, Emma (Lewis).*	December 24, 1908.	**13**, 512
Jones, Theodore.	*Miller, Addie Belle.*	September 13, 1915.	**16**, 439
Jones, Thomas.	*Jackson, Ida.*	June I5, 1905.	**12**, 206
Jones, Willie H.	*Bolden, Ora (Spears).*	October 21, 1911.	**15**, 109
Jones, Wilson Jr.	*Garland, Bessie.*	July 14, 1910.	**14**, 370
Jones, Wm.	*Carr, Emma.*	April 16, 1903.	**11**, 147
Junkins, Ira.	*Rhodes, Murril.*	December 3, 1913.	**16**, 15
Kelley, James.	*Boston, Minnie.*	October 3, 1910.	**14**, 414
King, Charles.	*Spears, Ora.*	May 25, 1917.	**17**, 173
King, Joseph Kirkland.	*Harris, Edith.*	July 7, 1918.	**17**, 395
Knox, Clemon L.	*Marshall, Ida.*	June 13, 1905.	**12**, 197
Lafura, Phillip.	*Smith, Lillie May.*	January 24, 1914.	**16**, 55
Lawery, Harry.	*Campbell, Florence.*	December 24, 1923.	**19**, 369
Lawson, Charles.	*Grever, Amand.*	September 24, 1902.	**OB 10**, 34
Lawson, Ellis.	*Johnson, Helen.*	July 10, 1916.	**16**, 622
Lawson, Leslie.	*Johnson, Maudie E.*	November 27, 1916.	**17**, 72
Lee, Clarence.	*Smith, Julia.* **W**	October 31, 1903.	**11**, 280
Lcc, Edward Walker.	*Saulsbury, Lulu Mary.*	January 17, 1907.	**13**, 70
Lee, Eugene.	*Lowry, Minnie S. (Coles).*	January 11, 1909.	**13**, 534
Lee, George.	*Jackson, Sallie (Bryant).*	May 11, 1918.	**17**, 362
Lee, Samuel A.	*Jenkins, Rose.*	December 12, 1920.	**18**, 319
Level, Ralph.	*Lee, Laura (Tutt).*	March 29, 1919.	**17**, 529
Lewis, Earl.	*Jones, Susie.*	September 27, 1926.	**20**, 228

Groom's name	*Bride's name (maiden)*	Marriage date	**Record Book** Page
Lewis, John H.	*Tolson, Myrtle.*	April 6, 1901.	**OB 10**, 12
Lewis, R.C.	*Waites, Gertrude.*	November 6, 1909.	**14**, 173
Lewis, Samuel.	*Burton, Elsie.*	July 27, 1924.	**19**, 472
Lewis, Thomas T.	*Strother, Mabel E.*	April 17, 1911.	**14**, 562
Lewis, W.W.	*Morris, Dollie Douglas (Rodgers).*	Sept. 29, 1920.	**18**, 272
Lewis, Walter.	*Langford, Hattie.*	December 14, 1903.	**11**, 331
Lewis, Wesley.	*Mease, Josephine Jessie (Pettiford).*	Dec. 26, 1904.	**12**, 71
Lighon, Ed.	*Graves, Ruth.*	August 17, 1911.	**11**, 218
Lighon, Thomas.	*Garland, Winnie May.*	May 16, 1906.	**12**, 463
Lipscomb, Robert.	*Underwood, Lizzie (Stevens).*	June 13, 1904.	**11**, 471
Logan, Charles.	*Douglass, Cleodose.*	August 26, 1903.	**11**, 225
Logan, Henry.	*Jackson, Missouri (Hodges).*	August 17, 1914.	**16**, 197
Logan, Tony.	*Holmes, Cora.*	April 6, 1904.	**11**, 425
London, Herbert B.	*Brown, Helen A.* **W**	August 5, 1918.	**17**, 471
Long, Joe Henry.	*Bates, Essie C. (Findley).*	August 12, 1912.	**15**, 296
Lopes, Peter P. **W**	*Delutz Hervey, Junniette S. (Champ).*	Jan. 14, 1915.	**16,** 294
Lopojne, John. **W**	*Frost, Josephine (Butts).*	September 17, 1918.	**17**, 438
Lowry, Lewis.	*Cole, Minnie.*	June 23, 1902.	**OB 10**, 32
Lukens, Charley J.	*Wild, Eleanor A. (Thomas).*	October 31, 1914.	**16**, 246
Madison, Archie.	*Cook, Judith.*	March 5, 1903.	**11**, 122
Malone, Wilkinson H.	*Jones, Anna.*	October 15, 1903.	**11**, 266
Mannel George.	*Reid, Carrie.*	October 4, 1905.	**12**, 269
Mardis, Scott Julian.	*Baker, Myron.*	October 17, 1918.	**17**, 457
Marie, Wm.	*Lewis, Fannie.*	April 24, 1920.	**18**, 159
Martin, Claude.	*Branch, Harriet (Carter).*	May 14, 1910.	**14**, 334
Mask, William H.	*Oliver, Essie.*	December 16, 1912.	**15**, 388
Mason, James.	*Johnson, Willie B.*	October 27, 1909.	**14**, 164
Mason, John W.	*Frazier, Lulu.*	July 31, 1904.	**11**, 499
Mathews, James.	*Russell, Mary (Weever).*	July 7, 1917.	**17**, 199
Mathews, Stewart.	*Logan, Mrs. Jennie (Welch).*	November 28, 1901.	**OB 10**, 21
Matthews, Frank R.	*Harvey, Osa May.*	July 22, 1905.	**12**, 230
Mays, Edward.	*Webb, Josephine.*	February 16, 1910.	**14**, 262
Mays, Leonard W.	*Washington, Anna M.*	July 25, 1914.	**16**, 186
McCarty, Wm.	*McCarty, Lulu (Thomas).*	July 6, 1918.	**17**, 393
McCormick, George.	*Hawkins, Hattie (Taylor).*	September 13, 1903.	**11**, 237
McCutcheon, W.H.	*Burton, Hattie.*	December 27, 1917.	**17**, 303
McDonald, James P.	*Birkett, Lydia.*	March 20, 1909.	**13**, 577

Groom's name	*Bride's name (maiden)*	Marriage date	**Record Book** Page
McDowell, Baxter.	*Lee, Mary E.*	November 30, 1906.	**13**, 42
McDowell, Baxter.	*Coleman, Grace.*	April 24, 1911.	**14**, 574
McKinley, John Anthony.	*Jones, Addie.*	June 16, 1904.	**11**, 474
McKinney, Alfred.	*Shoots, Amanda.*	March 12, 1923.	**19**, 177
McKinney, Thomas.	*Watkins, Elizabeth Frances.*	February 3, 1906.	**12**, 386
McMillan, Robert.	*Mitchell, Cora.*	June 25, 1907.	**13**, 170
Mead, Charles.	*Crump, Isabella (Cisoir).*	October 5, 1918.	**17**, 447
Mealy, Alfonso.	*Grooms, Anna (Blanchard).*	November 6, 1925.	**20**, 80
Mealy, William O.	*Rue, Elizabeth (Whaley).* **W**	October 1, 1903.	**11**, 252
Mealy, William Oscar.	*Statmire, Agnes (Curry).*	January 17, 1920.	**18**, 85
Medley, Arthur.	*Johnson, Ella (Toliver).*	September 24, 1916.	**17**, 19
Medley, Lee.	*Walker, Emma.*	September 20, 1926.	**20**, 227
Merrill, John.	*Taylor, Julia Mrs.*	September 25, 1907.	**13**, 217
Mese, Jackson.	*Harris, Celia (Antony).*	April 23, 1904.	**11**, 438
Michael, James L.	*Calvin, Cora (Ferguson).*	February 16, 1906.	**12**, 400
Mickens, Ephraim.	*Wheeler, Carrie.*	September 27, 1909.	**14**, 140
Miles, Clefton.	*Miles, Minta (Johnson).*	December 7, 1923.	**19**, 352
Miller, Brisco.	*Gaines, Susan A. (Walters).* **W**	July 19, 1905.	**12**, 228
Miller, Cornelius B.	*Smith, Julia M.*	January 1, 1910.	**14**, 228
Miller, George A.	*Hatton, Pearl.*	August 9, 1905.	**12**, 238
Miller, John Thomas.	*Michiel, Rosa.*	November 11, 1915.	**16**, 462
Miller, Wallace.	*Cason, Vergie.*	July 10, 1922.	**19**, 29
Miller, William F.	*Davis, Celery S. (Martin).*	March 24, 1908.	**13**, 330
Mitchell, Gabe.	*Cruse, Alice.*	August 31, 1904.	**11**, 526
Mitchell, Thomas.	*Chocklote, Grace.*	February 8, 1915.	**16**, 306
Mitchell, Thomas W.	*Coleman, Lorna (Wilson).*	December 24, 1921.	**18**, 568
Moffett, John J.	*Lewis, Josephine.*	May 25, 1904.	**11**, 459
Monroe, James T.	*Young, Lillie Lee.*	September 29, 1906.	**12**, 559
Monteen, Arthur.	*Valentine, Georgia.*	September 16, 1906.	**12**, 545
Montgomery, Thomas E.	*Flournay, Naomi N.*	September 28, 1903.	**11**, 251
Moore, Benjamin H.	*Woods, Ollie.*	June 25, 1911.	**15**, 36
Moore, John W.	*Turner, Georgia (Jones).*	June 30, 1904.	**11**, 486
Moore, Lewis.	*Turner, Viola.*	May 4, 1909.	**14**, 37
Moore, Lloyd.	*Brighton, Lulu.*	April 10, 1905.	**12**, 151
Moore, Peter.	*Boyer, Daisey.*	December 24, 1907.	**13**, 277
Morgan, Allan A.	*Lee, Sadie B.*	May 25, 1903.	**11**, 172
Morris, Lewis.	*Hollingsworth, Feddie.*	November 22, 1903.	**11**, 300
Morris, Lewis.	*Harris, Ida.*	March 5, 1910.	**14**, 281

Groom's name	*Bride's name (maiden)*	Marriage date	**Record Book** Page
Morrison, Geo. D.	*Howell, Beatrice.*	April 8, 1917.	**17**, 136
Morrison, George.	*Cleo Nicholson.* **W**	October 10, 1915.	**16**, 445
Morrison, Paul J.	*Washington, Leon.*	August 20, 1921.	**18**, 486
Morrison, W.C.	*Gray, Mabel (Nickelson).* **W**	September 19, 1921.	**18**, 506
Morrison, William C.	*Wright, Georgia.*	June 13, 1910.	**14**, 351
Moseley, Peter.	*Mozee, Anna (Woods).*	September 25, 1909.	**14**, 138
Mosley, Luke M.	*Neila, May Ellen (Powell).*	March 4, 1909.	**13**, 565
Moss, Artie.	*Thompson, Kate.*	October 28, 1903.	**11**, 276
Neal, James H.L.	*Taylor, Lillian.*	July 16, 1906.	**12**, 500
Nelson, Archie.	*Jefferson, Cora L.*	December 27, 1909.	**14**, 220
Nelson, James A.	*Nelson, Isebell "Sarah" (Jackson).*	August 11, 1904.	**11**, 513
Newsome, Rufus.	*White, Anna Margurite.*	March 21, 1906.	**12**, 433
Nicholas, Henry.	*Green, Bertha.*	June 8, 1907.	**13**, 155
Nicholas, Joseph W.	*Francis, Nora E.*	January 7, 1911.	**14**, 500
Nicholas, Joseph W.	*Truss, Georgia.*	May 23, 1914.	**16**, 142
Nolan, Lewis Robert.	*Cogan, Murrel.* **W**	June 18, 1913.	**15**, 545
Nolan, Thomas.	*Nelson, Cora.*	October 20, 1903.	**11**, 270
Oliver, O.C. **W**	*Graves, Mary Ethel.*	December 23, 1922.	**19**, 124
Oliver, Richard.	*Bickley, Mamie E. (Allen).*	May 16, 1910.	**14**, 333
Oliver, William.	*Hill, Nettie.*	May 28, 1902.	**OB 10**, 29
Owens, Henry.	*Campbell, Allie.*	September 22, 1924.	**19**, 505
Palmer, W. H.	*Harris, Margaret Alice.*	August 31, 1901.	**OB 10**, 20
Parker, Henry J.	*Flowers, Alberta.*	November 2, 1908.	**13**, 474
Parker, Mack.	*Stevenson, Bertha.*	September 29, 1909.	**14**, 144
Parker, Wiley.	*Mays, Mary.*	November 27, 1903.	**11**, 316
Patterson, Alexander.	*Tansil, Lillian.*	April 27, 1911.	**14**, 578
Patterson, Samuel.	*Tolbert, Bessie.*	November 9, 1915.	**16**, 461
Payne, Robert.	*Johnson, Alice May.*	June 4, 1912.	**15**, 266
Peacoe, Samuel H.	*Hamilton, Lulu (Weaver).*	October 3, 1905.	**12**, 267
Penn, William Calvin.	*Reasby, Nora (Gilbert).*	November 14, 1917.	**17**, 258
Pertillo, Walter.	*Harvey, Addie L. (Lewis).*	September 22, 1904.	**11**, 547
Peterson, Oscar.	*Hooker, Mary.*	September 25, 1906.	**12**, 548
Pettigrew, Jessie.	*Mickens, Anna.*	March 23, 1917.	**17**, 132
Phillips, Lewis D.	*Spears, Jenneive.*	December 26, 1914.	**16**, 276
Phillips, Lewis David.	*Spears, Genevieve.*	November 9, 1918.	**17**, 465
Pinson, James William.	*Dysart, Opal Olivia.*	December 14, 1926.	**20**, 255
Porter, Ethel.	*Berry, Willis.*	October 24, 1904.	**11**, 574

Groom's name	*Bride's name (maiden)*	Marriage date	**Record Book** Page
Price, John W.	*Gilbert, Flora.*	November 26, 1910.	**14**, 454
Price, William C.	*Jones, Edith H.*	April 2, 1923.	**19**, 182
Quails, Robert.	*Bryson, Mary "Lee".*	January 4, 1915.	**16**, 287
Quinn, Levi P.	*Rhodes, Hattie.*	December 21, 1922.	**19**, 117
Ramsey, Jenks Linn.	*Gaines, Nettie Gertrude.*	December 30, 1903.	**11**, 353
Randolph, Chas.	*Laster, Anna (Hinton).*	March 28, 1923.	**19**, 180
Randolph, William T.	*Moore, Addie.*	June 4, 1910.	**14**, 344
Ratliff, Ampsted J.	*Brown, Daisy Belle.*	November 30, 1904.	**12**, 16
Reasby, James E.	*Montjoye, Le Doshya (Mardes).*	February 14, 1920.	**18**, 106
Reasby, Jesse Hernadon.	*Curry, Massie.*	February 12, 1903.	**11**, 97
Reasby, Lewis.	*Hamilton, Rena (Alston).*	September 21, 1911.	**15**, 89
Beasby, Walker.	*Dooley, Catharine.*	January 11, 1923.	**19**, 137
Reasby, William.	*Wright, Gertrude.*	March 5, 1919.	**17**, 517
Reasby, William Lewis.	*Washington, Verbena Belle.*	June 23, 1908.	**13**, 392
Reed, Chas.	*Williams, Mrs. Maggie (Walker).*	November 20, 1920.	**18**, 300
Reynolds, Ester.	*Lewis, Malinda.*	November 11, 1908.	**13**, 483
Rhodes, Charles J.	*Thomas, Ruth.*	January 16, 1904.	**11**, 363
Rhodes, Henry.	*Burse, Mary Ella (Rucker).*	May 25, 1902.	**OB 10**, 29
Rhodes, Henry M.	*Strange, Annie (Bates).*	May 29, 1906.	**12**, 469
Rhodes, James.	*Taylor, Eldora.*	December 2, 1903.	**11**, 322
Rhodes, James.	*Stuart, Lula.*	July 1, 1915.	**16**, 397
Rhodes, John Porter.	*Daugherty, Rosaet.*	November 25, 1901.	**OB 10**, 22
Rhodes, Sam.	*Spears, Bernice.*	September 21, 1912.	**15**, 317
Rhodes, Samuel Jr.	*Washington, Hallie.*	February 25, 1920.	**18**, 120
Richey, Andrew.	*Jones, Estella.*	July 3, 1906.	**12**, 494
Ricks, Scott.	*Bawes (Bowers?), Julia (Tate).*	September 15, 1909.	**14**, 129
Riley, William.	*Woodfork, Millie.*	March 12, 1906.	**12**, 425
Ritchie, John.	*Gaines, Myrtle.*	September 11, 1907.	**13**, 207
Roach, John Frank.	*Williams, Maggie (Carr).*	August 19, 1916.	**17**, 5
Roach, Roderick.	*Watkins, Maggie.*	October 25, 1920.	**18**, 290
Roades, Gilmo.	*Wilson, Rena Bell.*	March 24, 1905.	**12**, 137
Roberts, Myrl.	*Green, Maggie (Warren).*	July 12, 1920.	**18**, 224
Roberts, William Fritz.	*Morris, Estella Mary (Brown).*	June 17, 1911.	**15**, 34
Robinson, Ed.	*Coles, Carrie.*	September 30, 1913.	**15**, 604
Robinson, Edward.	*Walker, Maggie.*	March 2, 1906.	**12**, 418
Robinson, James.	*McLaughlin, May (Cartwright).*	**W** March 27, 1916.	**16**, 557
Robinson, John.	*Smith, Sally.*	October 20, 1903.	**11**, 269

Groom's name	*Bride's name (maiden)*	Marriage date	**Record Book** Page
Robinson, John.	*Wheeler, Ethel.*	January 25, 1912.	**15**, 179
Robinson, John H.	*Douglass, Maud (Steele).*	February 17, 1906.	**12**, 401
Robinson, Joseph L.	*Harper, Mabel Mrs.*	October 26, 1905.	**12**, 292
Robinson, Loyd.	*Walker, Sarah (Lawson).*	February 15, 1920.	**18**, 102
Robinson, Thomas.	*Barbee, Lena.*	November 12, 1908.	**13**, 479
Robinson, Thomas C.	*Francis, Nora Mae.*	August 23, 1915.	**16**, 423
Rodrignez, Nolberta Garcia.	*Glen, Mrs. Maggie Belva (Adams).*	January 12, 1920.	**18**, 82
Rogers, James E.	*Lynch, Beulah.*	August 26, 1915.	**16**, 428
Roman, John Thomas.	*Woods, Mrs. Mary (Cobbs).*	November 22, 1921.	**18**, 545
Rose, Rufus.	*Bassett, Daisey.*	February 6, 1907.	**13**, 85
Ross, Charles H.	*Marshall, Martha (Cwena).*	November 6, 1906.	**13**, 19
Ross, Dave.	*Graves, Jennie.*	June 1, 1918.	**17**, 375
Ross, Lorenzo D.	*Holman, Myrtle M.*	December 23, 1905.	**12**, 347
Rowland, Clinton.	*Stowers, Mattie.*	November 1, 1906.	**13**, 17
Rowley, George E.	*Davis, Sadie.*	August 30, 1911.	**15**, 78
Russell, Henry.	*Allen, Ella.*	May 15, 1901.	**OB 10**, 14
Russell, Martin O.	*Ferguson, Josephine.*	December 16, 1903.	**11**, 333
Sandridge, Henry.	*Webster, Katie (Hill).*	May 24, 1909.	**14**, 45
Saunders, Charles J.	*Jackson, Carrie.*	November 1, 1902.	**11**, 20
Scott, David.	*Bradshaw, Angeline (Atkinson).*	April 7, 1923.	**19**, 192
Scott, Harry F.	*Winston, Clara Ella.*	January 1, 1902.	**OB 10**, 29
Scott, L. R.	*Edmonds, Viola.*	November 16, 1916.	**17**, 56
Scott, L.R.	*Stewart, Nettie (Finks).*	July 26, 1924.	**19**, 473
Scott, William E.	*Burton, Willie M.*	October 26, 1904.	**12**, 4
Scroggin, Sim.	*Cooper, Sadie Thomas.*	May 22, 1918.	**17**, 369
Sears, Harry.	*McDowell, Emma.*	February 22, 1922.	**18**, 600
See, Charley.	*Larkin, Betty.*	June 13, 1924.	**19**, 445
Sellers, Walter.	*Buford, Leona.*	April 24, 1923.	**19**, 162
Shaffer, Walter.	*Wilson, Mattie.*	June 23, 1903.	**11**, 190
Shelton, Charles.	*Burris, Mary (Bell).*	March 15, 1905.	**12**, 133
Shelton, Richard.	*Givens, Elizabeth (Overton).*	December 2, 1916.	**11**, 78
Shelton, S. H.	*Ellis, Olie.*	February 27, 1915.	**16**, 322
Shelton, Soloman.	*Davis, Virgie.*	April 15, 1907.	**13**, 126
Shepherd, William J.	*Martin, Mary Lue.*	July 12, 1905.	**12**, 207
Simes, General Gibbons A.	*Reynold, Mrs. Mollie (Canada).*	August 18, 1915.	**16**, 419
Simmons, Samuel.	*Vanarsdale, Laurabelle.*	March 28, 1927.	**20**, 292
Simmons, Spencer C.	*Brazelton, Ola W.*	June 12, 1912.	**15**, 271
Simms, Issac.	*Allen, Rosa (Hamilton).*	January 2, 1924.	**19**, 377

Groom's name	*Bride's name (maiden)*	Marriage date	**Record Book** Page
Sims, Doe S.	*Glenn, Ida E.*	July 14, 1916.	**16**, 626
Sims, General.	*Donaldson, Flora.*	July 23, 1921.	**18**, 470
Smith, Clarence C.	*Crank, Harriett I.*	November 11, 1914.	**16**, 252
Smith, Daniel.	*Zimmerman, Grace.*	April 1, 1911.	**14**, 553
Smith, Earnest.	*Grimes, Stella (Claybourne).*	January 23, 1928.	**28**, 395
Smith, Elijah P.	*Sager, Anna (Smith).*	June 1, 1904.	**11**, 466
Smith, Garland M.	*Reeves, Oakley Mae.*	December 8, 1919.	**18**, 53
Smith, Hart.	*Ely, Mary E.*	November 30, 1904.	**12**, 31
Smith, Leaman.	*Morrison, Georgia (Blackman).*	October 30, 1926.	**20**, 243
Smith, Thomas.	*Robinson, Henrietta.*	May 15, 1901.	**OB 10**, 13
Smith, W. M.	*Laster, Ollie B.*	April 13, 1910.	**14**, 312
Smith, William.	*Garland, Elizabeth.*	February 11, 1911.	**14**, 522
Smith, William A.	*Washington, Emma (Arther).*	November 6, 1912.	**15**, 362
Smith, William Andrew.	*Douglas, Nannie May.*	August 19, 1901.	**OB 10**, 17
Smith, William S. A.	*Lindsey, Emma.*	October 2, 1905.	**12**, 265
Smith, William Thomas.	*Rhodes, Margaret.*	October17, 1907.	**13**, 231
Solobillings, Joshua Louie.	*Wilson Mae Ida "Merida".*	October 22, 1916.	**17**, 44
Sorrell, George.	*Dizel, Eliza.*	February 24, 1903.	**11**, 112
Sorrell, Joseph.	*Graves, Frances (Jones).*	June 12, 1911.	**15**, 31
Spears, William.	*McQuerry, Eula May.*	February 15, 1927.	**18**, 364
Speers, Rudolph.	*Pinson, Maudbelle.*	March 26, 1921.	**20**, 290
Spencer, Reuben T.	*Martin, Ella.*	July 23, 1904.	**11**, 494
Spencer, Robert.	*Minder, Mary.*	August 11, 1905.	**12**, 239
Spicer, Thomas E.	*Jones, Susannah.*	March 20, 1907.	**13**, 108
Stallsworth, L. W.	*Davis, Anna.*	January 3, 1905.	**12**, 79
Stanton, Lee A.	*Wellington, Georgianna (Grimes).*	Dec. 28, 1910.	**14**, 492
Staples, James A.	*Smith, Maggie.*	May 27, 1903.	**11**, 173
Staten, A. M.	*Taylor, Ethel D. (Mitchell).*	December 19, 1917.	**17**, 294
Step, Virgil T.	*Terrell, Stella.*	August 29, 1911.	**15**, 76
Stevenson, Homer C.	*Carter, Hester H.*	July 17, 1918.	**17**, 400
Steveson, Frank.	*Bell, Lizzie.*	March 27, 1902.	**OB 10**, 27
Stewart, Rev. James W.	*Finks, Nettie.*	December 22, 1918.	**17**, 481
Stokes, Washington.	*Turner, Rhoda/Rosia.*	September 29, 1911.	**15**, 95
Stone, Robert.	*Brent, Icy.*	August 12, 1901.	**OB 10**, 17
Stoutmire, John.	*Curry, Agnes.*	May 16, 1918.	**17**, 366
Stovaul, Andrew.	*Edwards, Maude.*	February 24, 1909.	**13**, 561
Sykes, Rufus.	*Benson, Maudilena.*	March 13, 1909.	**13**, 576
Sykes, Rufus.	*Powell, Jennie (Watson).*	November 11, 1918.	**17**, 466

Groom's name	*Bride's name (maiden)*	Marriage date	**Record Book** Page
Tansil, Earl.	*Bon, Vergie B.L. (Davis).*	January 31, 1912.	**15**, 183
Tate, Albert.	*Ellis, Ollie.*	June 8, 1910.	**14**, 349
Tate, Benjamin F.	*Ampy, Edna.*	November 4, 1903.	**11**, 286
Tate, Harvey.	*Reasby, Mrs. Gertrude (Wright).*	August 16, 1923.	**19**, 267
Tate, Joseph.	*Gipson, Littie.*	December 23, 1902.	**11**, 56
Tate, Logan.	*Garland, Viola M. (Reeser).* **W**	March 8, 1911.	**14**, 540
Taylor, John H.	*Winston, Ella.*	April 11, 1903.	**11**, 139
Taylor, Warren.	*Yancy, Selena.*	December 2, 1903.	**11**, 319
Taylor, William M.	*Brown, Annie (McDade).*	June 7, 1921.	**18**, 433
Taylor, William S.	*Maril, Viola (Owens).*	December 25, 1912.	**15**, 403
Thomas, Allen.	*Thomas, Senora (Jackson).*	October 11, 1922.	**19**, 74
Thomas, Herbert.	*Burkett, Maggie.*	September 3, 1919.	**17**, 628
Thomas, John.	*Stevenson, Bertha.*	May 19, 1904.	**11**, 455
Thomas, John.	*Agee, Bessie (Gathers).*	December 16, 1906.	**13**, 48
Thomas, John T.	*Williams, Mary (Crider).*	August 25, 1923.	**19**, 278
Thomas, Pearl.	*Smith, Virginia.*	April 16, 1912.	**15**, 234
Thomas, Robert.	*Jones, Bessie (Garland).*	January 27, 1919.	**17**, 498
Thompson, Albert.	*Perkins, Dorothy.*	November 8, 1917.	**17**, 254
Thompson, Marion.	*Woods, Carrie.*	April 21, 1904.	**11**, 435
Thompson, Monroe.	*Mason, Lena (Gibson).*	December 26, 1905.	**12**, 354
Thornton, Robert.	*Hoston, Ethel.*	May 31, 1918.	**17**, 371
Timlic, Andrew C.	*Mason, Lulu (Frazier).*	September 25, 1907.	**13**, 216
Tobin, James.	*March, Emma Thompson.*	October 4, 1921.	**18**, 515
Tole, William.	*Graves, Mary E.*	January 13, 1904.	**11**, 359
Tolson, Charles Guy.	*Brown, Jessie Lee.*	November 17, 1915.	**16**, 467
Tolson, R.T.	*Kitchens, Birdie.*	June 17, 1920.	**18**, 203
Toran, Edward.	*Bates, Eliza.*	February 21, 1912.	**15**, 201
Truby, George Henry.	*Maxwell, Rebecca Jane.*	July 19, 1906.	**12**, 502
Tucker, J.D.	*Holmes, Anna (Bauks).*	December 10, 1921.	**18**, 559
Turner, Alford L.	*Green, Elizabeth (McCann).*	September 16, 1921.	**18**, 503
Turner, Charles.	*Williams, Bettie (Johnson).*	April 28, 1910.	**14**, 325
Turner, Enoch.	*Camper, Elizabeth.*	July 28, 1914.	**16**, 187
Turner, Enoch.	*Lee, Ella (Battles).*	September 23, 1918.	**17**, 441
Turner, Eugene.	*Tolson, Maggie B.*	May 11, 1909.	**14**, 41
Turner, George E.	*Bradshaw, Blanch.*	March 25, 1911.	**14**, 548
Turner, Howard Venston.	*Burkes, Leona.*	January 27, 1915.	**16**, 301
Turner, William Henry.	*Spears, Jennievie.*	January 6, 1910.	**14**, 229

Groom's name	*Bride's name (maiden)*	Marriage date	**Record Book** Page
Underwood, Reeves.	*Jones, Henrietta.*	April 28, 1901.	**OB 10**, 13
Vance, Albert.	*Anderson, Alice.*	March 12, 1904.	**11**, 402
Vanderver, William.	*Tolson, Olive.*	April 2, 1904.	**11**, 420
Wade, Columbus.	*Smith, Virginia.*	March 28, 1907.	**13**, 110
Wade, John H.	*Elgan, Parthena Mrs. (Jones).*	October 5, 1908.	**13**, 222
Wade, Robert.	*Rucker, Ada.*	August 7, 1908.	**13**, 419
Waites, Daniel.	*Reasby, Pauline Mrs.*	March 16, 1907.	**13**, 106
Walden, Harry W.	*Cary, Australia.*	August 29, 1906.	**12**, 531
Walker, Alexander.	*Edmonds, Irene.*	November 9, 1929.	**20**, 635
Walker, Charlie Hurndon.	*James, Eva.*	December 17, 1904.	**12**, 61
Walker, George.	*Rucker, Anna.*	April 3, 1905.	**12**, 143
Walker, Nelson.	*Arnold, Susie.*	April 4, 1904.	**11**, 421
Walker, Walter.	*Watson, Lulu.*	April 28, 1923.	**19**, 216
Wallington, Edward.	*Bluff, Minerva.*	July 7, 1905.	**12**, 210
Walls, Eldist.	*Lewis, Jenette E.*	September 27, 1917.	**17**, 233
Walters, George W.	*Young, Norma (Kelso).*	May 18, 1919.	**17**, 552
Ware, Louie.	*Edmonds, May (Robinson).*	October 11, 1919.	**18**, 11
Warricks, William Porter.	*Cousins, Hazeldel.*	April 30, 1913.	**15**, 482
Washington, William O.	*Allen, Hazel A.*	November 16, 1915.	**16**, 472
Washington, Wm. Jr.	*Faidley, Eva.*	February 24, 1923.	**19**, 163
Watkins, Gus.	*Carter, Bella.*	September 3, 1901.	**OB 10**, 17
Watkins, Sedan J.	*Doyle, Minnie L.*	March 24, 1914.	**16**, 101
Watkins, Thomas.	*Carr/Cary, Bertha (Perkins).*	March 30, 1912.	**15**, 222
Watson, Martin.	*Matthews, Mary (Grever).*	November 22, 1926.	**20**, 251
Watson, Orville.	*Poindexter, Nellie.*	June 18, 1913.	**15**, 540
Weaver, Lewis.	*Getter, Clara.*	February 9, 1903.	**11**, 94
Webb, Theodore.	*Bonner, Florence (Logan).*	November 13, 1915.	**16**, 466
Webster, Fredric Douglas.	*Randolph, Carrie B.*	November 28, 1917.	**17**, 270
Webster, Jeese J.	*Garland, Fannie (Brooks).*	April 25, 1921.	**18**, 406
Weeks, William McKinley.	*Lewis, Sadie Naomi.*	June 29, 1920.	**18**, 213
Welch, Emanuel.	*Saunders, Naomi.*	June 3, 1911.	**15**, 23
Wellington, Joe D.	*Shavers, Della.*	December 23, 1913.	**16**, 27
Wesley, Lonnie.	*Furgeson, Leona.*	December 1, 1925.	**20**, 92
West, Frank Jr.	*Graves, Sadie.*	May 29, 1922.	**19**, 8
West, Lenord.	*Payne, Margaret.*	February 17, 1919.	**17**, 510
Weston, James.	*Higgins, Lucille.*	October 21, 1922.	**19**, 84
Weston, William.	*Rogers, Marie.*	May 30, 1905.	**12**, 184
Wheeler, Authur W.	*Jones, Mary Alice.*	June 1, 1918.	**17**, 372

Groom's name	*Bride's name (maiden)*	Marriage date	**Record Book** Page
Wheels, Delbert.	*Brown, Jeanetta.*	September 26, 1925.	**20**, 69
Wheels, Oscar.	*Reasby, Martha.*	May 15, 1918.	**17**, 365
Wheels, William.	*Doyle, Mattie.*	January 11, 1916.	**16**, 507
Whisiker, Samuel W.	*Wilson, Emma.*	May 1, 1905.	**12**, 169
White, Allen.	*Edwards/Edmonds, Lulu E.*	December 26, 1918.	**17**, 486
White, James C.	*Coleman, Nannie.*	January 3, 1907.	**13**, 65
White, Timothy W.	*Holland, Maggie.*	December 9, 1900.	**OB 10**, 7
Whitler, John A.	*Harvey, Elnora.*	May 30, 1914.	**16**, 149
Williams, Charles.	*Steele, Beatrice.*	June 28, 1905.	**12**, 214
Williamson, Henry.	*Guy, Vergie.*	August 23, 1923.	**19**, 276
Williams, Amos.	*White, Myrtle.*	August 8, 1904.	**11**, 509
Williams, Arthur.	*Hoggsett, Virginia.*	February 25, 1911.	**14**, 530
Williams, Cecil.	*Jones, Anna.*	July 9, 1922.	**19**, 30
Williams, Earl.	*Beaman, Warnetta.*	March 12, 1921.	**18**, 378
Williams, George.	*Johnson, Mrs. Fannie (Mickens).*	January 10, 1917.	**17**, 100
Williams, George L.	*Mason, Lue.*	June 1, 1904.	**11**, 465
Williams, J. L.	*Faulkner, Mabel (Holley).*	May 24, 1926.	**20**, 164
Williams, Jack W.	*Colley, Charilty.*	January 13, 1919.	**17**, 492
Williams, John.	*Porter, Maud.*	January 2, 1901.	**OB 10**, 10
Williams, John W.	*Faidley, Lillie M. (Frankland).*	August 29, 1911.	**15**, 75
Williams, Sidney.	*Smith, Maggie (Walton).*	September 28, 1907.	**13**, 219
Williams, William E.	*Harris, Emma.*	November 2, 1905.	**12**, 273
Williams, William E.	*Clark, Arvilla (Johnson).*	October 17, 1907.	**13**, 234
Willis, Linford R.	*Lucas, Ella Josephine (Mays).*	April 8, 1914.	**16**, 114
Wilson, Arthur.	*Taylor, Minnie.*	December 13, 1904.	**12**, 56
Wilson, Clarence.	*Curtaindall, Almena.*	February 21, 1912.	**15**, 204
Wilson, Clark A.	*Moore, Mabel E.*	April 23, 1911.	**14**, 571
Wilson, Horace.	*King, Ruby.*	December 30, 1909.	**14**, 227
Wilson, Jacob.	*Truss, Lizzie.*	December 31, 1902.	**11**, 62
Wilson, Luke R.	*Jackson, Dora.*	February 15, 1906.	**12**, 398
Wimsey, June.	*Rose, Ruby.*	December 10, 1922.	**19**, 111
Windfield, James D.	*Jackson, Eva.*	February 17, 1904.	**11**, 386
Winfield, James D.	*Underwood, Elizabeth (Stevens).*	October 26, 1905.	**12**, 289
Winfree, A. G.	*Johnson, Addie (Logan).*	September 12, 1918.	**17**, 437
Woodlord, Charles.	*Jordon, Marie.*	January 3, 1921.	**18**, 339
Woodford, Isaac.	*Downs, Sarah M. (Wood).*	June 6, 1922.	**19**, 12
Woodford, Sam.	*Rumley, Julia.*	July 1, 1920.	**18**, 216

Groom's name	*Bride's name (maiden)*		Marriage date	**Record Book** Page
Woodford, Ushaw.	*Bates, Josephine.*		March 27, 1907.	**13**, 113
Woodley, Ed.	*Burkett, Lydia.*		January 10, 1920.	**18**, 79
Woods, Walter A.	*Cobbs, Mary.*		December 12, 1905.	**12**, 339
Woods, William.	*Collins, Mary.*		August 2, 1900.	**OB 10**, 4
Wright, Arthur.	*Snead, Mary Ann.*		April 24, 1901.	**OB 10**, 13
Wright, Clyde.	*Burton, Priscilla.*		October 29, 1924.	**19**, 527
Wright, Gus W.	*Allen, Lucey B.*		December 10, 1902.	**11**, 45
Wright, John Wesley Alex.	*Bailey, Henrietta Polk.*		April 6, 1905.	**12**, 146
Wright, Richard.	*Faidley, Lulu.*		November 28, 1910.	**14**, 456
Wright, William.	*Floyd, Pearl (Lewis).*		August 13, 1910.	**14**, 394
Yancey, Judge D.	*Barber, Mrs. Eva.*		July 11, 1914.	**16**, 178
Yancy, G. D.	*Rowland, Mattie.*	**W**	December 25, 1917.	**17**, 298
Yates, Ernest.	*Woodson, Beatrice.*		October 23, 1909.	**14**, 160
Young, Charley J.	*Morris, Neal.*		December 24, 1914.	**16**, 272

The White House Hotel, Buxton. (Monroe County Historical Museum.)

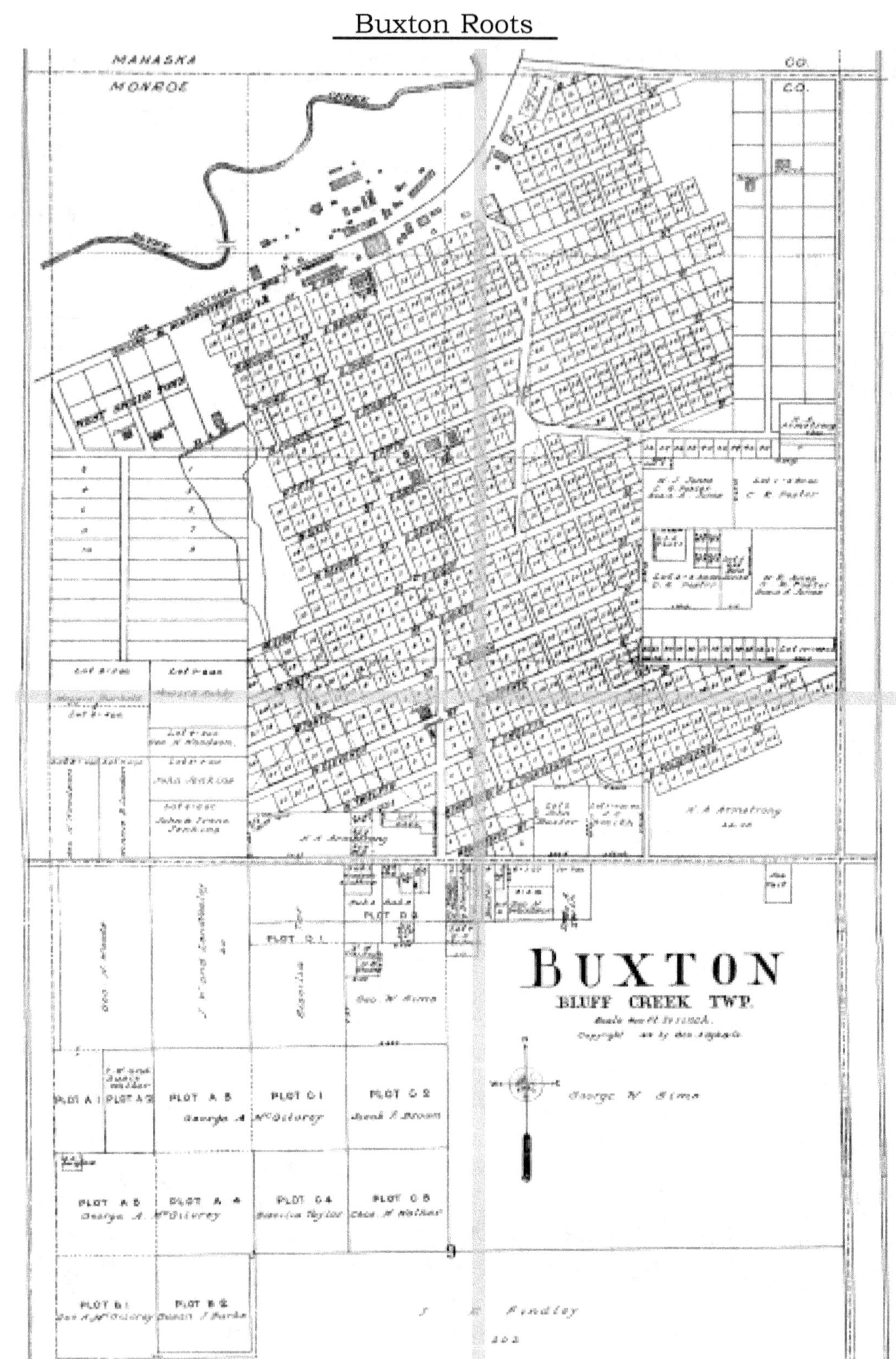
MAHASKA
MONROE
CO.
CO.
BUXTON
BLUFF CREEK TWP.
PLOT A 1
PLOT A 2
PLOT A 3
PLOT C 1
PLOT C 2
PLOT A 5
PLOT A 4
PLOT C 4
PLOT C 3
PLOT B 1
PLOT B 2
PLOT D 1
PLOT D 2
George W. Sims
J. R. Findley
9

Buxton Census 1910

Records of who lived in which house have been assembled from the 1910 Federal Census of Monroe County, Iowa. Spellings are copied as they were written on the census document. Occupations are included where available. The map at left shows the entire town; enlargements are on following pages.

House #	Street	Name	Occupation (if available)
23	East 14th Street	James T. Parkin	
19	East 14th Street	Junie Tate	
19	East 14th Street	Logan Tate	
14	East 14th Street	George W. Vanansdale	
14	East 14th Street	James Marshall	
13	East 14th Street	Bert McDowell	
12	East 14th Street	John Holland	
12	East 14th Street	Lonnie Carter	
12	East 14th Street	Prizella Carter	
12	East 14th Street	Isabella Carter	
12	East 14th Street	James Carter	
12	East 14th Street	Fredie Carter	
12	East 14th Street	Ida Carter	
11	East 14th Street	James Wignall	
10	East 14th Street	George W. Norris	
10	East 14th Street	William H. Brown	
9	East 14th Street	James Henry	
9	East 14th Street	Reese Williams	
9	East 14th Street	Emma Williams	
8	East 14th Street	John H. Davies	
8	East 14th Street	Charles Brown	
7	East 14th Street	Fred Betson	
6	West 14th Street	William Strider	
6	West 14th Street	Jackson Brookins	
6	West 14th Street	Alonzo T. Watson	
5	West 14th Street	Charles Green	
5	West 14th Street	Ushaw Woodford	
7	West 14th Street	John Wade	
7	West 14th Street	Inez Miller	
7	West 14th Street	Emma Miller	
1	East 13th Street	Lucas Winkler	
2	East 13th Street	Abraham Hatchett	
7	East 13th Street	Emerson Doyle	
7	East 13th Street	Charles Dabney	
8	East 13th Street	Benjamin Jones	

(census listing continues on page 44)

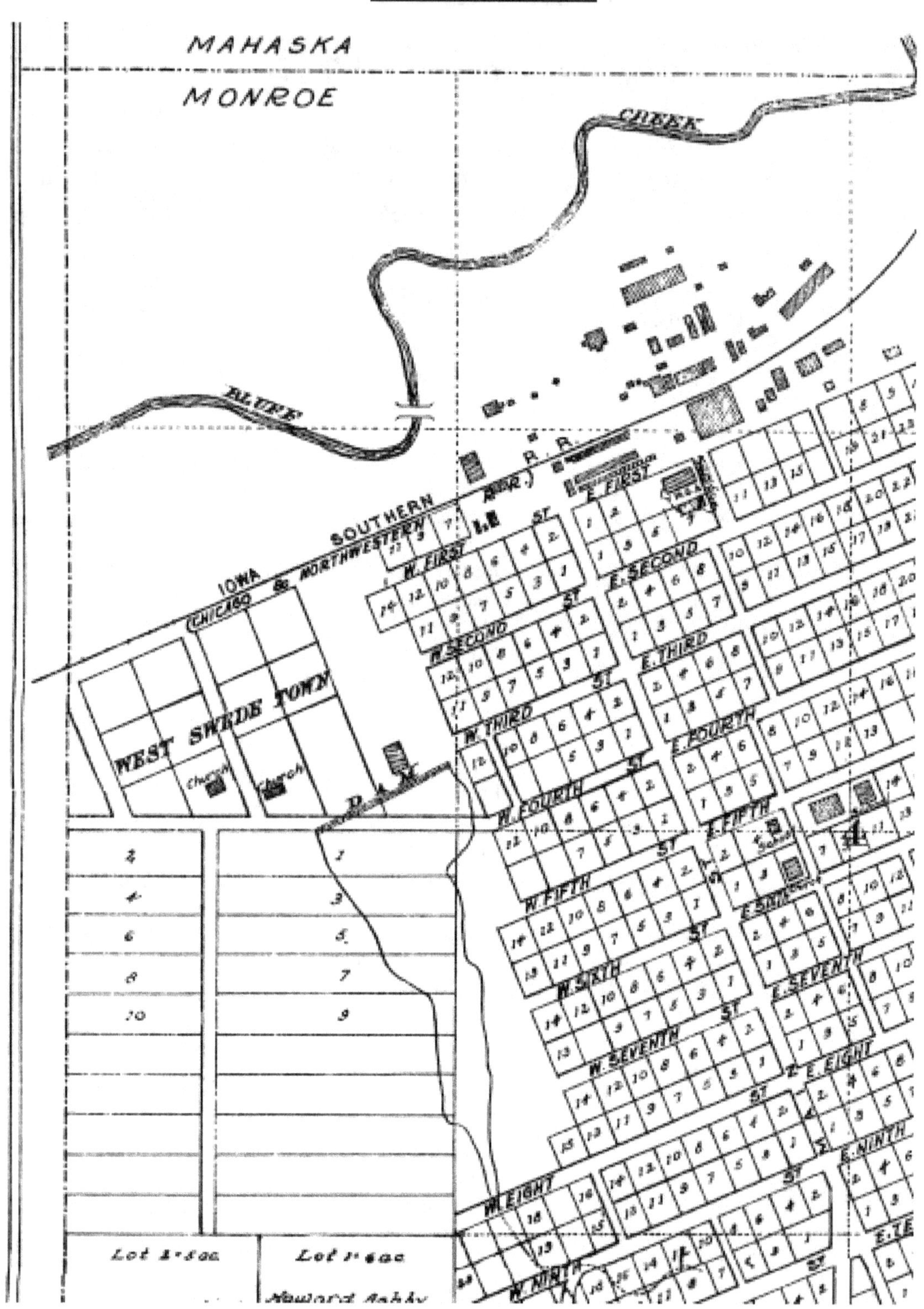
MAHASKA
MONROE
CREEK
BLUFF
IOWA
SOUTHERN
CHICAGO & NORTHWESTERN
R.R.
WEST SWEDE TOWN
Church
Church
W. FIRST
ST
E. FIRST
E. SECOND
W. SECOND
E. THIRD
W. THIRD
E. FOURTH
W. FOURTH
E. FIFTH
W. FIFTH
W. SIXTH
E. SEVENTH
W. SEVENTH
E. EIGHT
W. EIGHT
E. NINTH
W. NINTH
Lot 1 & 2 ac.

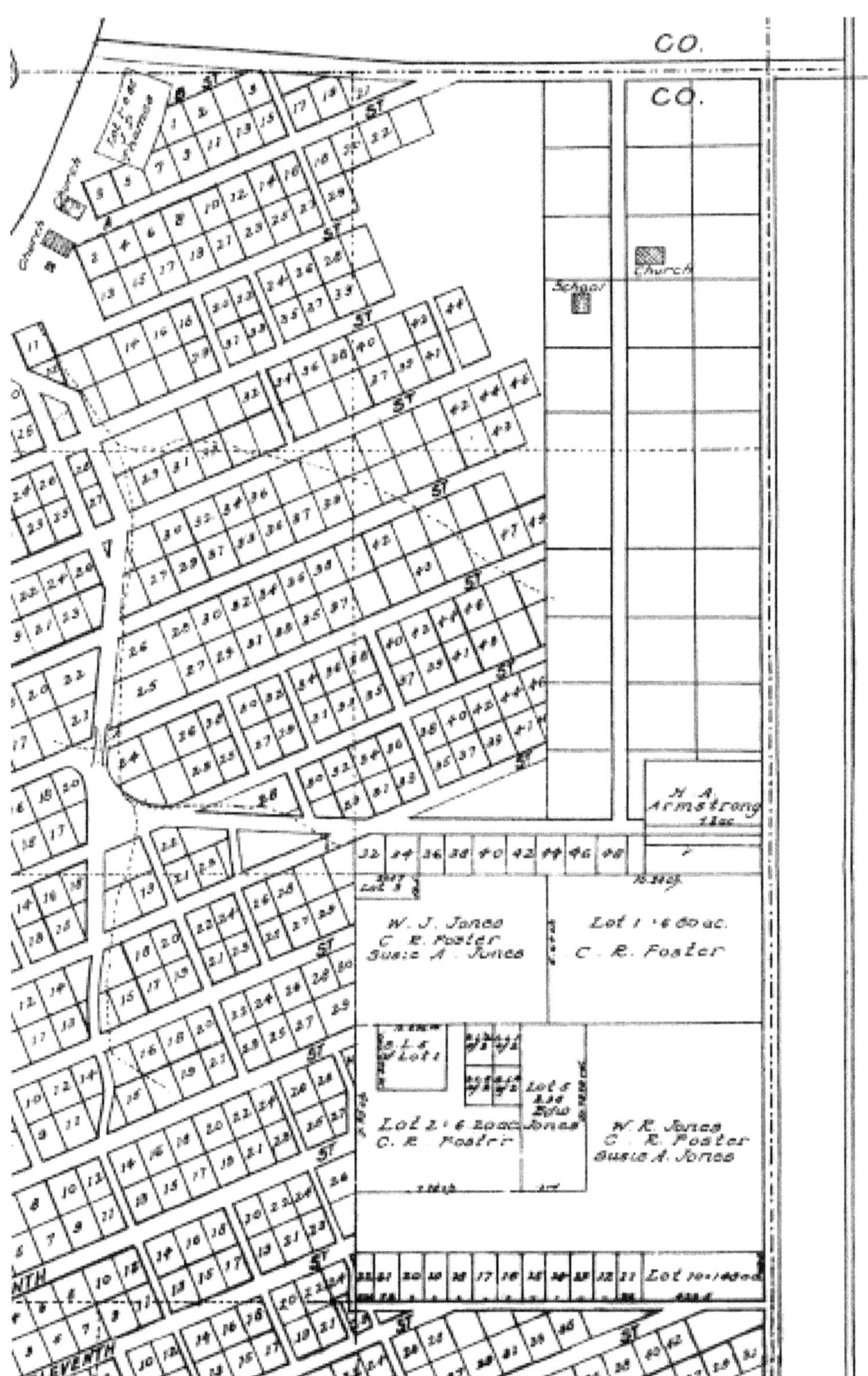
CO.
CO.
Church
School
Church
H. A. Armstrong
W. J. Jones
C. R. Foster
Susie A. Jones
C. R. Foster
W. R. Jones
C. R. Foster
Susie A. Jones
ELEVENTH

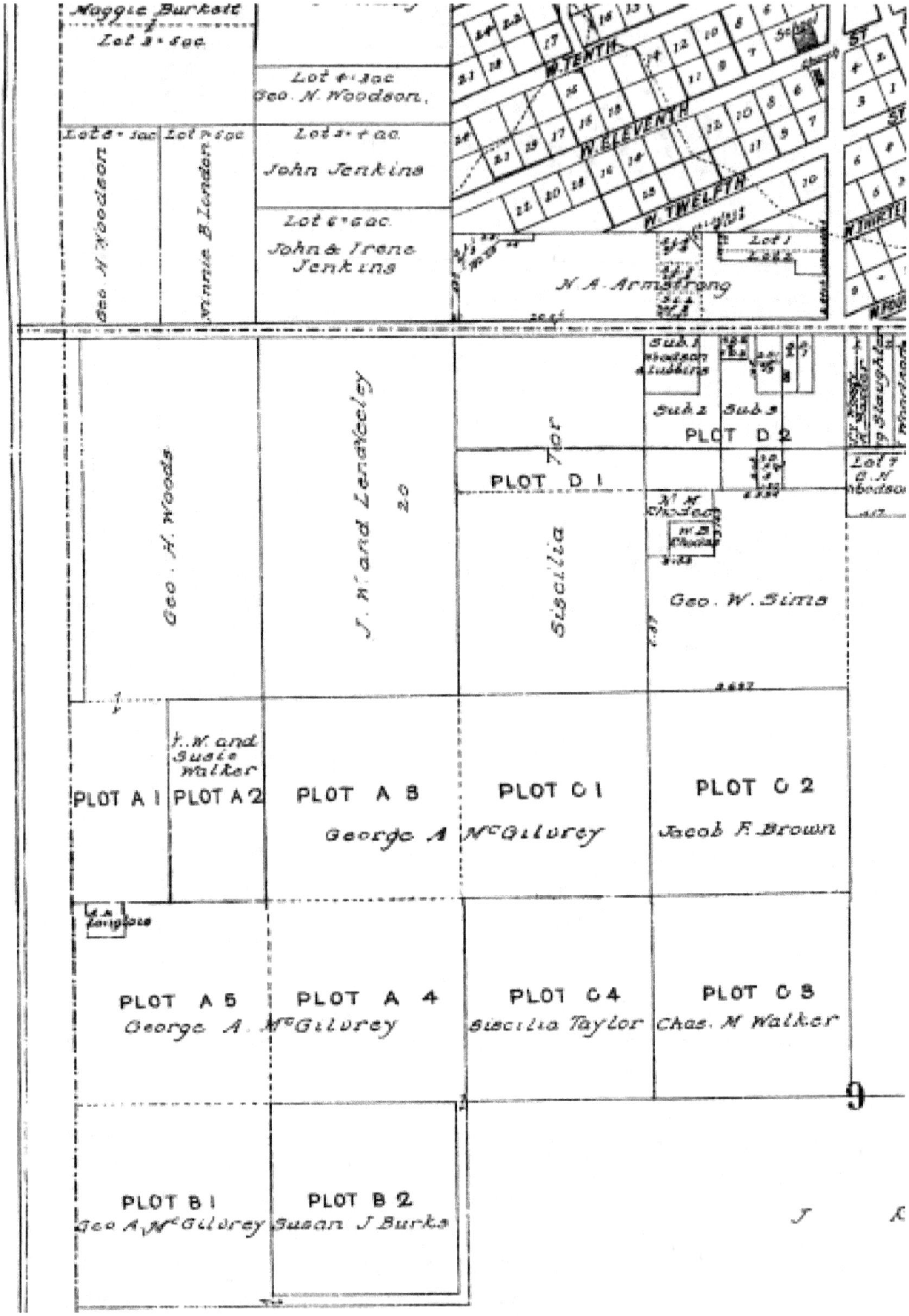
Maggie Burkett
Lot 3 • 5ac
Lot 4 • 3ac
Geo. N. Woodson.
Lot 8 • 3ac
Lot 7 • 5ac
Lot 5 • 4 ac.
John Jenkins
Lot 6 • 5ac.
John & Irene Jenkins
Geo. H Woodson
Winnie B London
W. TENTH
W. ELEVENTH
W. TWELFTH
School
N. A. Armstrong
Lot 1
Sub 1
Sub 2
Sub 3
PLOT D 2
PLOT D 1
Lot 7
G. H Woodson
Geo. H. Woods
J. W. and Lendaeley
20
Siscilia Taylor
Geo. W. Sims
J. W. and Susie Walker
PLOT A 1
PLOT A 2
PLOT A 3
George A McGilvrey
PLOT C 1
PLOT C 2
Jacob F. Brown
PLOT A 5
George A. McGilvrey
PLOT A 4
PLOT C 4
Siscilia Taylor
PLOT C 3
Chas. M Walker
9
PLOT B 1
Geo A McGilvrey
PLOT B 2
Susan J Burks

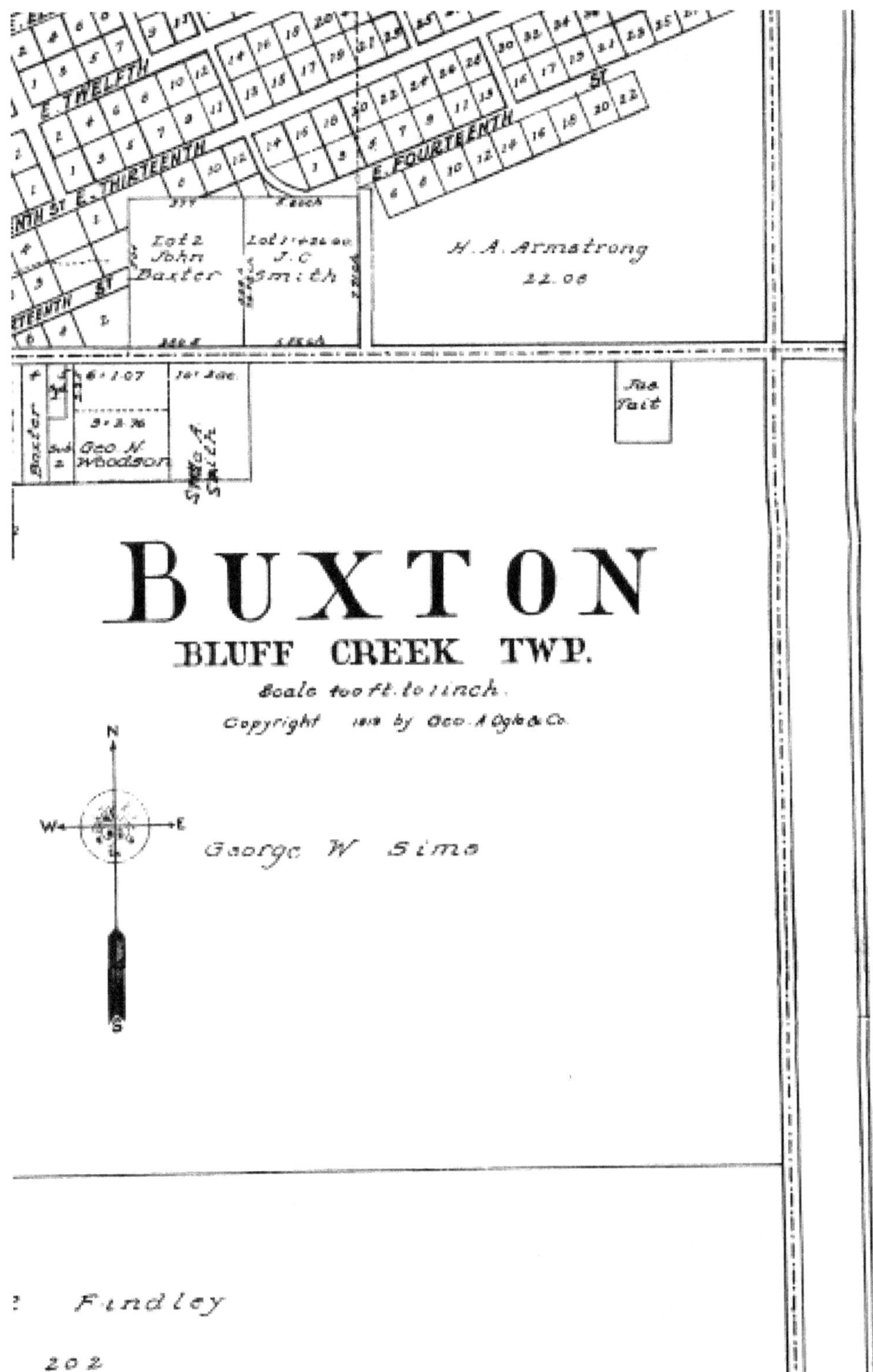

E. TWELFTH
E. THIRTEENTH
E. FOURTEENTH
ST
Lot 2 John Baxter
Lot 1 J. C. Smith
H. A. Armstrong
22.08
Geo N. Woodson
Baxter
Jas Tait
BUXTON
BLUFF CREEK TWP.
Scale 400 ft. to 1 inch.
Copyright 1919 by Geo. A Ogle & Co.
N
W
E
S
George W Sims
Findley
202

8	East 13th Street	Rachel Mury	
9	East 13th Street	Willie Cross	
10	East 13th Street	Jules Vandemerlen	
12	East 13th Street	Cres Miller	
12	East 13th Street	Mary Miller	
14	East 13th Street	Anderson March	
18	East 13th Street	John H. Taylor	
19	East 13th Street	Joseph A. Delong	
20	East 13th Street	Edward Fincher	
21	East 13th Street	Joseph A. Fincher	
21	East 13th Street	Sadie Jones	
21	East 13th Street	Harry Fincher	
22	East 13th Street	John Maughan	
24	East 13th Street	William Boston	
24	East 13th Street	Minnie Boston	
24	East 13th Street	Clarence Boston	
24	East 13th Street	Susie Chaffee	
28	East 13th Street	Sampson Phillips	
28	East 13th Street	Mattie Barlow	
28	East 13th Street	Matthew Barlow	
28	East 13th Street	Hattie Coleman	
28	East 13th Street	Richard Coleman	
34	East 13th Street	Julia Ricks	Boardinghouse
34	East 13th Street	Vance Harris	
34	East 13th Street	John Harris	
34	East 13th Street	Walter Bowers	
34	East 13th Street	Joanna Bowers	
34	East 13th Street	Millard Tate	
34	East 13th Street	Sidney Tate	
33	East 13th Street	Henry Clay	
33	East 13th Street	Flora Wilson	
33	East 13th Street	Ruth Wilson	
33	East 13th Street	Lizzie Brent	
36	East 13th Street	William Darden	
36	East 13th Street	Julia Brown	
30	East 13th Street	Henry Jones	
1	West 13th Street	John Mashak	
2	West 13th Street	Frank Raskotnik	
5	West 13th Street	Robert Hart	
2	East 12th Street	Agne Ceglar	
2	East 12th Street	John Palcic	
2	East 12th Street	John Tursic	
1	East 12th Street	John Essinger	
3	East 12th Street	William Richards	

LeeAnn Dickey

4	East 12th Street	Robert Cobbs	
5	East 12th Street	Charley Cross	
6	East 12th Street	Rice Ellis	
7	East 12th Street	Clay Funk	
8	East 12th Street	John Baker	
10	East 12th Street	John Bienchi	
11	East 12th Street	Antone Veolar	
11	East 12th Street	Thomas Ray	
11	East 12th Street	Lucy Griffin	
11	East 12th Street	Phillips Burk	
12	East 12th Street	Charley Anderson	
12	East 12th Street	Blanch M. Wood	
13	East 12th Street	William Hocking	
13	East 12th Street	Alfred Hall	
13	East 12th Street	Sam Coty	
14	East 12th Street	Andrew Jefferson	
14	East 12th Street	Archie Nelson	
14	East 12th Street	James H. Nelson	
15	East 12th Street	Walter Hocking	
15	East 12th Street	Florence Hocking	
15	East 12th Street	Mary Parkin	
15	East 12th Street	George Parkin	
15	East 12th Street	William Griffiths	
15	East 12th Street	William Simpson	
16	East 12th Street	Clint Steveson	
16	East 12th Street	Bertha Parker	Furniture Store Bookkeeper
16	East 12th Street	Leonard L. Walker	
18	East 12th Street	Martin Lee	
19	East 12th Street	Clarence Taylor	
19	East 12th Street	Elnora Freeman	Dress Maker
19	East 12th Street	Earl Freeman	
20	East 12th Street	John Hanstrom	
22	East 12th Street	Hiram Wright	
22	East 12th Street	Seskel Johnson	
23	East 12th Street	James Estes	Butler- Private Family
23	East 12th Street	Edgar McCoy	
26	East 12th Street	Charles H. Ross	
28	East 12th Street	Frank Woods	
1	West 12th Street	Joseph Yesse	
1	West 12th Street	Fredric Kullniz	
1	West 12th Street	John Janeka	
1	West 12th Street	George Brocerns	
2	West 12th Street	Frank Assinger	
3	West 12th Street	Oscar T. Tansil	
4	West 12th Street	William Morgan	
4	West 12th Street	John T. Morgan	

6	West 12th Street	Isiah Lewis	
6	West 12th Street	Roscoe C. Lewis	
7	West 12th Street	George Taylor	
10	West 12th Street	James Harvey	
10	West 12th Street	Pinkie L. Epperson	
10	West 12th Street	Robert S. Hooper	
11	West 12th Street	Sidney Williams	
11	West 12th Street	Cesial Smith	
11	West 12th Street	Frank Hombles	
15	West 12th Street	Andrew Pivosarnik	
15	West 12th Street	Joe Broz	
4	West 11th Street	Alex Tate	
4	West 11th Street	Austin Francis	
4	West 11th Street	Lee L. Epperson	Minister- Pastor
2	West 11th Street	Robert Southers	
1	West 11th Street	Green Poe	
6	West 11th Street	Hayes Hale	
6	West 11th Street	Amanda Trussels	
9	West 11th Street	Emery H. Hill	
10	West 11th Street	John Garland	
10	West 11th Street	Nellie Lash	
10	West 11th Street	William Dial	
10	West 11th Street	Ella Munzlock	
10	West 11th Street	William Walters	
10	West 11th Street	Mary Walters	
10	West 11th Street	Cora Momand	Laundress
14	West 11th Street	John Allen	
14	West 11th Street	John H. Allen	
15	West 11th Street	James Washington	
19	West 11th Street	William Washington	
19	West 11th Street	Scott Stribling	
19	West 11th Street	Laura White	
19	West 11th Street	Alvin C. Jackson	
19	West 11th Street	Herbert Jackson	
19	West 11th Street	William Jackson	
19	West 11th Street	Mattie Stribling	
2	East 11th Street	Vensall Hessler	
3	East 11th Street	Henry Graves	
3	East 11th Street	Dave Cole	
6	East 11th Street	Burton Creach	
6	East 11th Street	John Hubbard	
7	East 11th Street	John W. Mappin	
5	East 11th Street	Earl Houston	
9	East 11th Street	John DeWitt	
9	East 11th Street	Annie Dudgeon	Cook- Private Family

10	East 11th Street	Harry Parker	
11	East 11th Street	Charles Pugh	
11	East 11th Street	Ruth Pugh	Bakery-Bookkeeper
14	East 11th Street	John H. Watkins	
13	East 11th Street	Charles Stiggers	
15	East 11th Street	Charles Green	
16	East 11th Street	Jones Harold	
16	East 11th Street	Margaret Alexander	
17	East 11th Street	William Small	
20	East 11th Street	George F. Mash	
20	East 11th Street	Julia Newman	
20	East 11th Street	Milious Brannon	
19	East 11th Street	James D. Winfield	
19	East 11th Street	Ruth Underwood	
21	East 11th Street	Thomas J. Parkey	
22	East 11th Street	Phillip G. Thomas	
24	East 11th Street	Battres Burks	
24	East 11th Street	Allen Bucknor	
24	East 11th Street	George W. Mayes	Minister- Pastor
0	East 10th Street	Hattie Garrett	Saleswoman- Restaurant
0	East 10th Street	James Garrett	
1	East 10th Street	Longhorne Cheatham	
2	East 10th Street	Robert Hale	
3	East 10th Street	Newt Cary	
3	East 10th Street	Sam Bryant	
3	East 10th Street	Joe Garrett	
4	East 10th Street	Charles Brown	
5	East 10th Street	Harry Gewecke	
7	East 10th Street	George Martin	
10	East 10th Street	Nelson C. Pendleton	
11	East 10th Street	David J. Hayes	
11	East 10th Street	Mary Hayes	
11	East 10th Street	Myrtle Hayes	
13	East 10th Street	Albert Poston	
13	East 10th Street	Bessie Miller	
13	East 10th Street	Carrie Saunders	
13	East 10th Street	Johnnie Jackson	
14	East 10th Street	John Scott	
15	East 10th Street	Robert Johnson	
15	East 10th Street	Ella Wallace	Cook- Private Family
15	East 10th Street	Al Johnson	
16	East 10th Street	Charles Darden	
16	East 10th Street	Lucy Keith	
16	East 10th Street	Isaac Johnson	
16	East 10th Street	Flossie May Johnson	
18	East 10th Street	Charley Todd	

21	East 10th Street	James Smith	
24	East 10th Street	Dave DeWitt	
24	East 10th Street	Herbert Halford	
25	East 10th Street	Charley Butler	
26	East 10th Street	York Smith	
26	East 10th Street	Lula Ballard	
26	East 10th Street	Donzel Ballard	
26	East 10th Street	Charley E. Covington	Engineering- Steam
27	East 10th Street	Alfred Gordon	
1	West 10th Street	Westley Allen	
1	West 10th Street	Mary Brown	
2	West 10th Street	Sarah Walker	Boardinghouse
3	West 10th Street	James Walker	
3	West 10th Street	Charles Walker	
3	West 10th Street	Carri T. Hill	
3	West 10th Street	John Parker	
3	West 10th Street	Amelia Smith	Housekeeper- Boardinghouse
3	West 10th Street	Oscar Smith	
3	West 10th street	Willie Whitson	
3	West 10th Street	Charles Cooper	
4	West 10th Street	William P. Griffith	
4	West 10th Street	Adline Griffith	
4	West 10th Street	James Hayes	
5	West 10th Street	Green Jackson	
5	West 10th Street	Aruse Allen	
5	West 10th Street	Thomas Jones	
7	West 10th Street	Clarcy Webb	Dressmaker
7	West 10th Street	Georgiana Welington	Housekeeper- Private Family
7	West 10th Street	Howard Johnson	
8	West 10th Street	William H. Simmons	
8	West 10th Street	Charley W. Rodgers	
10	West 10th Street	George Montgomery	
10	West 10th Street	John McMann	
14	West 10th Street	Richard C. Britton	
13	West 10th Street	George Davies	
15	West 10th Street	George Patterson	
2	East 9th Street	Andrew J. Johnson	
3	East 9th Street	Jesse Allen	
3	East 9th Street	Walter Frazier	
4	East 9th Street	Andrew Howard	
5	East 9th Street	Richard Crute	
6	East 9th Street	Daniel W. Carter	
6	East 9th Street	Mattie E. Carter	School Teacher
6	East 9th Street	General J. Carter	
7	East 9th Street	Joseph Bradshaw	

LeeAnn Dickey

7	East 9th Street	Earnest Bradshaw	
7	East 9th Street	Lizzie Garland	
7	East 9th Street	Clarence Garland	
7	East 9th Street	Ruby Garland	
8	East 9th Street	William King	
8	East 9th Street	Isaac Erby	
12	East 9th Street	George Stewart	
14	East 9th Street	William Fielding	
14	East 9th Street	Walter Fielding	
15	East 9th Street	George W. Watts	
15	East 9th Street	William Hayes	
18	East 9th Street	Robert McDonald	
19	East 9th Street	Bettie Williams	Laundress
19	East 9th Street	Sesco Jackson	
19	East 9th Street	Ethel Jackson	
20	East 9th Street	Henry Ray	
21	East 9th Street	George McDonald	
23	East 9th Street	William Smith	
22	East 9th Street	Clara B. Bailey	
22	East 9th Street	Nelson Robinson	
22	East 9th Street	Robert Canaday	
22	East 9th Street	Charles Mead	
26	East 9th Street	William Prentice	
27	East 9th Street	Oliver Eaves	
27	East 9th Street	Thomas Miner	
28	East 9th Street	Charles Turner	
28	East 9th Street	Benjamin Abney	
29	East 9th Street	Sam Foster	
29	East 9th Street	Margaret Pane	
30	East 9th Street	George W. Carter	
30	East 9th Street	Stella Terrel	
1	West 9th Street	George Kocur	
1	West 9th Street	John Siszak	
2	West 9th street	Lewis Coleman	
5	West 9th Street	Pink Harreld	
5	West 9th Street	Charley Carroll	
6	West 9th Street	William Skipwith	Blacksmith
6	West 9th Street	Ophelia Chritian	
6	West 9th Street	Joseph Wellington	
6	West 9th street	Mary Camppor	Washerwoman- Private Family
7	West 9th Street	Lee Reynolds	
8	West 9th Street	Robert A. Booker	
9	West 9th Street	George Kelssar	
11	West 9th Street	Andrew Palyo	
12	West 9th Street	James Mc Donald	
12	West 9th Street	Victoria Medley	

12	West 9th Street	Octava Medley	
12	West 9th Street	Kattie Brown	
14	West 9th Street	John Ondr	
15	West 9th Street	James C. White	
16	West 9th Street	Birdia Jefferson	
16	West 9th Street	John Ocskar	
16	West 9th Street	John Kenak	
16	West 9th Street	George Yenco	
16	West 9th Street	Andrew Fedor	
16	West 9th Street	Stephen Piezal	
18	West 9th Street	Sam Toupeka	
18	West 9th Street	Adam Hareek	
18	West 9th Street	John Pleton	
19	West 9th Street	John Graves	
23	West 9th Street	John Boksos	
23	West 9th Street	Elizabeth Boksos	
23	West 9th Street	Andrew M. Beno	
1	East 8th Street	William H. Lee	
4	East 8th Street	Delilah Lee	School Teacher
4	East 8th Street	Chollie Harris	
4	East 8th Street	Walter Thornton	
5	East 8th Street	Cairo Ray	
6	East 8th Street	Harry Coles	
6	East 8th Street	Taylor Watson	
7	East 8th Street	John D. Spears	
7	East 8th Street	James Spears	Lawyer
7	East 8th Street	Jennie V. Turner	
7	East 8th Street	Melrose Turner	
7	East 8th Street	Rodolphas Turner	
9	East 8th Street	William Sutherland	
10	East 8th Street	John S. Mays	
11	East 8th street	James Jackson	
12	East 8th Street	George Martin	
13	East 8th Street	Lee Graves	
14	East 8th Street	Will Smith	
14	East 8th Street	Lucy M. Griffin	
14	East 8th Street	Georgia M. Smith	
14	East 8th Street	Harry Smith	
16	East 8th Street	Henry Carter	
16	East 8th Street	Saddie M. Qualls	
17	East 8th Street	Samuel Burkett	
17	East 8th Street	Lydia McDonald	
17	East 8th Street	Leonard McDonald	
19	East 8th Street	Frank Stewart	
20	East 8th Street	Josh Miller	

21	East 8th Street	Edward W. Howell	
22	East 8th Street	Robert Nelson	
22	East 8th street	Clara Nolan	
23	East 8th Street	Daniel M. Smith	
24	East 8th Street	William Vandivier	
24	East 8th Street	Robert Christian	
24	East 8th Street	Lizzie Brink	Dressmaker
25	East 8th Street	Nannie Cook	
28	East 8th Street	John T. Ward	
28	East 8th Street	Johnnie Moore	
1	West 8th Street	Frank Darnell	Carpenter
1	West 8th Street	Grace Clark	
2	West 8th Street	John M. Young	
3	West 8th Street	Henry Logan	
3	West 8th Street	Armanda Cunningham	
3	West 8th Street	Gracie Brown	
4	West 8th Street	William Carter	
5	West 8th Street	Sam S. Carter	
5	West 8th Street	Henry Brown	Fireman
6	West 8th Street	Joseph Hresko	
7	West 8th Street	Boyd Henry	
8	West 8th Street	Nora Francis	
8	West 8th Street	Andrew Vargsko	
8	West 8th Street	John Mesaros	
9	West 8th Street	Dan Clark	
9	West 8th Street	Carrie Clark	
9	West 8th Street	Casta Price	
12	West 8th Street	George Gogo	
13	West 8th Street	Dock S. Sims	
14	West 8th Street	George Kocur	
15	West 8th Street	William H. Britton	
16	West 8th Street	William Brooks	Blacksmith
1	East 7th Street	John R. Blaney	
3	East 7th Street	Lewis Davis	
4	East 7th Street	Mamie Banks	
4	East 7th Street	James Frith	
5	East 7th Street	John A. Baker	
5	East 7th Street	Clod McKiney	
5	East 7th Street	Thomas McKiney	
5	East 7th Street	Jackson McGuire	
6	East 7th Street	Leonard Curry	
6	East 7th Street	Nannie Curry	
7	East 7th Street	William H. Cooks	
7	East 7th Street	Murda Beason	School Teacher
7	East 7th Street	Nora M. Harris	School Teacher

8	East 7th Street	Gust Allen	
9	East 7th Street	Rilie Sales	
10	East 7th Street	Joe Banister	
10	East 7th Street	Robert Weaver	Tobacco Factory
11	East 7th Street	Moses Tandy	
11	East 7th Street	Charley Gordon	
12	East 7th Street	George Monsulock	
13	East 7th Street	Plase Coffer	
13	East 7th Street	John Coffer	
14	East 7th Street	Clara Goforth	
14	East 7th Street	Charley Sturn	
17	East 7th Street	Charles Leonard	Driver- Drayman
15	East 7th Street	Joseph Henley	
18	East 7th Street	Richard Anderson	
19	East 7th Street	Robert Givens	
19	East 7th Street	Rachel Scrutchin	
21	East 7th Street	Zack Hartwell	
22	East 7th Street	Green Martin	
23	East 7th Street	William Sharp	Shot Firer
23	East 7th Street	Larance Bryant	
24	East 7th Street	Fred Coats	
28	East 7th Street	Sam Moppin	Drayman- Teamster
28	East 7th Street	Lena Gay	
28	East 7th Street	John Jones	
29	East 7th Street	Robert Lowery	
31	East 7th Street	Phillip Burkett	
32	East 7th Street	William F. Anderson	
33	East 7th Street	John C. Rowellett	Drayman- Teamster
33	East 7th Street	Gertrude Rowellett	School Teacher
34	East 7th Street	John W. Shaffer	
37	East 7th Street	William E. Turner	
39	East 7th Street	Lewis Strather	
39	East 7th Street	Bertha Strather	Post Office Clerk
39	East 7th Street	Harry Strather	Hotel Porter
42	East 7th Street	Frank Chambers	
44	East 7th Street	Davis Carter	
48	East 7th Street	Harry Swinscoe	
38	East 7th Street	Charles H. Castner	Carpenter
1	West 7th Street	Bennie T. Crank	
2	West 7th Street	Joseph Tate	
3	West 7th Street	Addison Brooks	Blacksmith
4	West 7th Street	Gus W. Wright	
5	West 7th Street	Lewis S. Jackson	
5	West 7th Street	John W. Riggs	
6	West 7th Street	Ferdinand Smith	

LeeAnn Dickey

8	West 7th Street	John Kocur	
9	West 7th Street	Andy Webb	
10	West 7th street	Mike Lenger	
12	West 7th street	Lewis R. Nolan	
13	West 7th Street	Adolphus Gleason	
13	West 7th Street	Dan Woodson	Teamster- Railroad
13	West 7th Street	Monroe Adams	
14	West 7th Street	William Phillips	
1	East 6th Street	Lewis Blaney	
1	East 6th Street	Mamie Henderson	
3	East 6th Street	Frank B. Woodard	Minister- Pastor
4	East 6th Street	Lewis Toran	
4	East 6th Street	Hosanna L. Toran	
5	East 6th Street	Luella Ragsdale	
5	East 6th Street	Lea Medley	
5	East 6th Street	Robert Cary	
7	East 6th Street	William Williams	
8	East 6th Street	Henry J. Parker	
9	East 6th Street	Harry W. Rhodes	
9	East 6th Street	Charles Y. Robinson	Physician
10	East 6th Street	Charles L. Lawson	
10	East 6th Street	Henry Grever	
10	East 6th Street	David Horne	
11	East 6th Street	Daniel Jelks	
12	East 6th Street	Stephen Anderson	
13	East 6th Street	Frank Melton	
13	East 6th Street	Leonard Williams	
13	East 6th Street	James Carter	
14	East 6th Street	Hiram Price	
14	East 6th Street	Nathaniel Price	
15	East 6th Street	Gus Watkins	
15	East 6th Street	Matthew Taylor	
15	East 6th Street	Jacob Jefferson	
15	East 6th Street	Emma Floyd	Cook- Private Family
23	East 6th Street	James Wheels	
23	East 6th Street	Martha Wheels	Cook- Restaurant
29	East 6th Street	Edward N. Whitlock	
30	East 6th Street	Charles L. McCoy	
31	East 6th Street	John Gaspor	
32	East 6th Street	Perry M. Parson	Foreman- Coal Mine
32	East 6th Street	Edna C. Parson	Clerk- Office of Dept. Store
32	East 6th Street		Clerk- Confectionary
32	East 6th Street	Loyd O. Oscar	
32	East 6th Street	Nelse Ottis Oscar	
34	East 6th Street	Henry McCoy	Watchman- Coal Yards

34	East 6th Street	Jennie Cooper	
34	East 6th Street	James Glenn	Teamster- Dept. Store
35	East 6th Street	Gust Peterson	Machine Blacksmith
36	East 6th Street	Ned Pterson	
37	East 6th Street	Susie Parker	
37	East 6th Street	Walter Moore	
37	East 6th Street	Pauline Cox	
37	East 6th Street	Aubra Moore	
37	East 6th Street	Addie Moore	
37	East 6th Street	Lewis Moore	
37	East 6th Street	Bennie Moore	
37	East 6th Street	Mable Moore	
37	East 6th Street	John M. Cox	
37	East 6th Street	James E. Cox	
37	East 6th Street	James P. Parker	
39	East 6th Street	Loyd Moore	
39	East 6th Street	Charley Leby	
40	East 6th Street	Joseph Strather	
41	East 6th Street	Steven Kovahn	
41	East 6th Street	Frank Benitt	
43	East 6th Street	John Cohler	
46	East 6th Street	George D. Johnson	Teamster- Dept. Store
1	West 6th Street	Walter H. Harvey	
2	West 6th Street	Adolph W. Wilson	
3	West 6th Street	James Reasby	
4	West 6th Street	John W. Price	
4	West 6th Street	James Mason	
5	West 6th Street	Marshall Lowery	
5	West 6th Street	Elsie Lowery	Nurse- Private Family
6	West 6th Street	David Phillips	
6	West 6th Street	Lloyd Byers	
7	West 6th Street	Bookers Denes	
7	West 6th Street	Olonzo Brooks	
8	West 6th Street	John Rivers	
8	West 6th Street	Maggie Rivers	
8	West 6th Street	Joy Rivers	
9	West 6th Street	Youmon Black	
9	West 6th Street	Bailey Black	
9	West 6th Street	Arthur Black	
10	West 6th Street	Perry Benge	
11	West 6th Street	Warren T. Brigham	
11	West 6th Street	Earnest Dibrell	
12	West 6th Street	Jacob Wilson	
12	West 6th Street	Georgia Truss	
12	West 6th Street	Samuel Wilson	

LeeAnn Dickey

13	West 6th Street	Henry S. Owsley	
14	West 6th Street	Moses Gaines	
14	West 6th Street	Bettie Wilson	
14	West 6th Street	James Mitchell	Musician- Teacher
14	West 6th Street	George Petes	School Janitor
1	East 5th Street	Washington Cheatham	
1	East 5th Street	Elizza Cheatham	
2	East 5th Street	French Brown	
3	East 5th Street	Lewis Gibson	
4	East 5th Street	Joseph Baker	
4	East 5th Street	Cordelia Mitchell	
5	East 5th Street	Sallie Reasby	
5	East 5th Street	Mary Wright	
5	East 5th Street	Reed Penn	
5	East 5th Street	William Jackson	
9	East 5th Street	George Russell	
11	East 5th Street	Loyd Cheatham	
13	East 5th Street	Mamie Bickley	
13	East 5th Street	George Franklin	
14	East 5th Street	Daniel Waites	
16	East 5th Street	Altis Clemens	
17	East 5th Street	Peter Mosley	
18	East 5th Street	Charlie J. Rhodes	
20	East 5th Street	Ira Tarwater	
21	East 5th Street	Joseph Sorrell	
24	East 5th Street	William H. Carter	
24	East 5th Street	James Nichols	
24	East 5th Street	Mark O. Russell	
24	East 5th Street	Jonnie Hughes	
25	East 5th Street	Lon McCurtis	
25	East 5th Street	William M. McMurray	
26	East 5th Street	James Bolton	
26	East 5th Street	William Cathcart	
27	East 5th Street	Richard R. Curtis	
27	East 5th Street	Flossie Massey	
28	East 5th Street	James Wheels	
29	East 5th Street	James Spade	
29	East 5th Street	Clyde Tucker	
30	East 5th Street	Oscar Peterson	
32	East 5th Street	George Dixon	
33	East 5th Street	George H. Hughes	
35	East 5th Street	Albert C. Hurst	
37	East 5th Street	Zelma Hurst	
37	East 5th Street	Thomas Watson	
37	East 5th Street	Robert Wade	
42	East 5th Street	William Flick	

43	East 5th Street	Arthur Carpenter	
46	East 5th Street	Charles Jones	
46	East 5th Street	Bessie Garland	
47	East 5th Street	Morgan Harris	
47	East 5th Street	Joseph Ball	
47	East 5th Street	Authur Ball	
49	East 5th Street	Thomas J. Gibbons	
1	West 5th Street	Albert H. Welington	Blacksmith- Company Shop
1	West 5th Street	George Welington	Blacksmith- Own Shop
3	West 5th Street	Matt Yanesy	
3	West 5th Street	Judge Yanesy	
4	West 5th Street	Hal Burford	
5	West 5th Street	Sam Prentice	
6	West 5th Street	Joseph C. Jones	
6	West 5th Street	John Young	
6	West 5th Street	Daniel Haynes	
7	West 5th Street	Rufus Newsom	Blacksmith- Company Shop
7	West 5th Street	Elviria Newsom	
7	West 5th Street	Matt Bolden	
8	West 5th Street	George Bock	
8	West 5th Street	Joseph Koffman	
10	West 5th Street	Andrew Gasper	
12	West 5th Street	Andrew Bins	
14	West 5th Street	John Kocker	
14	West 5th Street	George Intol	
1	East 4th Street	James F. Baker	Printer- Company Office
1	East 4th Street	Robert Qualls	
3	East 4th Street	George Lee	
3	East 4th Street	John Farrall	Insurance Agent
4	East 4th Street	Henry Burns	
5	East 4th Street	Wesley Garnett	
5	East 4th Street	Sam William	
6	East 4th Street	Alex Reeves	
6	East 4th Street	Okla M. Reeves	
6	East 4th Street	Virgil Stepp	
7	East 4th Street	Calvin Thomas	
7	East 4th Street	Emma Mitchell	
9	East 4th Street	Luke Wilson	
9	East 4th Street	Bernice Jackson	
9	East 4th Street	Payton Branch	
9	East 4th Street	Henry Bryant	
10	East 4th Street	Henry Hawkins	
12	East 4th Street	Booker Jones	

The mine superintendent's house. (Monroe County Historical Museum.)

Buxton street scene. (Monroe County Historical Museum.)

12	East 4th Street	Fannie Braxton	
13	East 4th Street	Mike Katusa	
14	East 4th Street	Joe Stiner	
16	East 4th Street	Wallace Miller	
16	East 4th Street	James Parker	
16	East 4th Street	Charles Brinker	
16	East 4th Street	Girelia Carry	
17	East 4th Street	James Ross	
17	East 4th Street	Annie Freeman	Washerwoman
17	East 4th Street	Georgia Wright	Waitress- Restaurant
18	East 4th Street	Peter Moore	
18	East 4th Street	Preston Boyers	
19	East 4th Street	Meredith Grandison	
19	East 4th Street	John F. Roache	
19	East 4th Street	Rodric Roache	
19	East 4th Street	John Roache	
20	East 4th Street	Bell L. Bates	
20	East 4th Street	Albert Railsy	
21	East 4th Street	Andrew Oliver	
21	East 4th Street	Osie W. Oliver	
21	East 4th Street	Cecil Oliver	
22	East 4th Street	Sam Scroggins	
23	East 4th Street	Annie Richey	
27	East 4th Street	Thomas Mc Donald	
28	East 4th Street	Lewis Wright	
29	East 4th Street	Arthur Hall	
30	East 4th Street	John W. Moore	
30	East 4th Street	Alfred Turner	
30	East 4th Street	George Turner	
30	East 4th Street	William Turner	
30	East 4th Street	Jessie Turner	
30	East 4th Street	Charley Jones	
32	East 4th Street	Will Aldridge	
32	East 4th Street	Bishop Smith	
32	East 4h Street	Frank Toran	
32	East 4th Street	Edward Toran	
33	East 4th Street	Willie L. Turner	
33	East 4th Street	Blanchie Bradshaw	Washerwoman- Private Family
34	East 4th Street	George Neal	
34	East 4th Street	Harry Neal	
34	East 4th Street	James Brooks	
34	East 4th Street	Mable Reasby	
35	East 4th Street	Fountain Guy	
35	East 4th Street	Margaret Amky	
35	East 4th Street	David Amky	
35	East 4th Street	George Amky	

35	East 4th Street	Duffie Amky	
35	East 4th Street	Hazel Braxton	
37	East 4th Street	William T. Reed	
37	East 4th Street	William Harker	
39	East 4th Street	Reuben T. Jones	
39	East 4th Street	Ollie Gordon	
39	East 4th Street	Wilson Carey	
42	East 4th Street	Nelson Walker	
42	East 4th Street	Beverly Walker	
43	East 4th Street	Charley Davis	
1	West 4th Street	Miles Carey	
1	West 4th Street	Ada Monroe	
1	West 4th Street	Floyd Monroe	Manager Pool Hall
4	West 4th Street	George D. Yancy	
6	West 4th Street	John Manosic	
6	West 4th Street	Julia Manosic	
6	West 4th Street	George Antolik	
6	West 4th Street	George Kotch	
6	West 4th Street	Mike Saber	
8	West 4th Street	William J. Sheperd	
8	West 4th Street	Joseph Martin	
10	West 4th Street	John Kupuster	
10	West 4th Street	John Olichena	
1	East 3rd Street	Stewart Mathews	
2	East 3rd Street	Aurdry Logan	
2	East 3rd Street	Unnamed Hicks	
3	East 3rd Street	Henry Reasby	
3	East 3rd Street	Milton Atkinson	
3	East 3rd Street	Amity Blakey	
4	East 3rd Street	Joseph Spears	
4	East 3rd Street	Lighting Thomas	
5	East 3rd Street	Charley Shelton	Fireman- Powerhouse
7	East 3rd Street	Charles N. Carter	
8	East 3rd Street	Walter Blaney	Salesman- Dept. Store
9	East 3rd Street	William A. Brown	Secretary- YMCA
9	East 3rd Street	Anna Brown	Music Teacher- School
10	East 3rd Street	Nannie Smith	Boardinghouse
10	East 3rd Street	Leona Taylor	
10	East 3rd Street	Richard Wright	
10	East 3rd Street	William Henry	
10	East 3rd Street	Lewis Lowery	
11	East 3rd Street	Frank Zabuder	
13	East 3rd Street	Charles Burgs	
13	East 3rd Street	Felik Raspotnik	

13	East 3rd Street	Jessie Burns	
13	East 3rd Street	Katie Burns	
14	East 3rd Street	Ned Robinson	Church Janitor
16	East 3rd Street	Wiley Parker	
16	East 3rd Street	John Mays	
16	East 3rd Street	Fannie Mays	
16	East 3rd Street	Walter Mays	
16	East 3rd Street	Floyd Mays	
16	East 3rd Street	Roscoe Mays	
16	East 3rd Street	Robert Mays	Street Newsboy
17	East 3rd Street	William H. Taylor	
17	East 3rd Street	Andrew Blakey	
17	East 3rd Street	George W. Burks	
18	East 3rd Street	John M. Carr	
18	East 3rd Street	Eck Carr	
19	East 3rd Street	William J. Jackson	
19	East 3rd Street	Mayme Finley	School Teacher
19	East 3rd Street	Annette Sharp	Dressmaker
20	East 3rd Street	Charles Hicks	
20	East 3rd Street	Zellar Brown	
21	East 3rd Street	Mary Mickens	
22	East 3rd Street	Sallie Jackson	
22	East 3rd Street	Ira DeSleet	
22	East 3rd Street	Morris DeSleet	
22	East 3rd Street	Georgia DeSleet	
23	East 3rd Street	Harce Wilson	
23	East 3rd Street	Deliah Smith	
24	East 3rd Street	Sherman Hogsette	
25	East 3rd Street	Rice Barber	
25	East 3rd Street	Eva Hunley	
27	East 3rd Street	Floyd Jones	
27	East 3rd Street	Virginia Hogsette	
27	East 3rd Street	Olaf P. Hogsette	
27	East 3rd Street	Charley Hogsette	
29	East 3rd Street	Dick Johnson	
30	East 3rd Street	Richard Johnson	
30	East 3rd Street	John A. Harris	Fireman- Stationary
31	East 3rd Street	John W. Lewis	
31	East 3rd Street	Elmer Carey	
32	East 3rd Street	Mary Woodford	
32	East 3rd Street	Mildridge Riley	
32	East 3rd Street	Zachriah Taylor	
33	East 3rd Street	Frank Lynch	
33	East 3rd Street	Duncan Johnson	
36	East 3rd Street	Robert H. Jones	
36	East 3rd Street	Walter Byers	

36	East 3rd Street	Haden Byers	
36	East 3rd Street	Hazel Walker	
36	East 3rd Street	Enoch Turner	
36	East 3rd Street	Virgial Hunter	
No #	East 3rd Street	Leonard A. Roberts	
No #	East 3rd Street	Arthur Roberts	Blacksmith- Own Shop
No #	East 3rd Street	Susan R. Harris	
37	East 3rd Street	Edwin Hart	
39	East 3rd Street	Edward Peterson	
41	East 3rd Street	Charles E. Stone	Yard Master- Railroad
42	East 3rd Street	William S. Jones	
44	East 3rd Street	George W. brooks	
46	East 3rd Street	John Fowler	
1	West 3rd Street	Frank Gustafson	
1	West 3rd Street	Christiana Ellison	
1	West 3rd Street	David Swanson	Laborer- Machine Shop
2	West 3rd Street	Lottie Swanson	
2	West 3rd Street	Ruth Swanson	Clerk Coal Office
3	West 3rd Street	Lewis Reasby	
3	West 3rd Street	Anna Jackson	Cook- Private Family
4	West 3rd Street	Hugh Pollock	
5	West 3rd Street	Andrew Kapal	
6	West 3rd Street	Thomas Lighon	Shot Firer
7	West 3rd Street	John Chunko	
7	West 3rd Street	Steven Kubresck	
8	West 3rd Street	Stewart Bingham	
8	West 3rd Street	William Jewett	
9	West 3rd Street	William H. Cozzens	Deputy Sheriff
9	West 3rd Street	Aaron Cozzens	
10	West 3rd Street	Nick Massey	
11	West 3rd Street	Edward Mills	Postmaster
11	West 3rd Street	James Mills	Janitor- YMCA
11	West 3rd Street	Authur Mills	Clerk- Pot Office
12	West 3rd Street	Lewis Robinson	
12	West 3rd Street	Peter Reeves	
1	East 2nd Street	Herman Anspach	Salesman- Dept. Store
2	East 2nd Street	Robert Hocking	
2	East 2nd Street	Simon Brandt	
2	East 2nd Street	Andrew Palitsch	
2	East 2nd Street	Lewis Galler	
2	East 2nd Street	Mushias Drausniz	
2	East 2nd Street	Lewis Hoffman	
3	East 2nd Street	Hugh Hastings	Salesman- Dept. Store
4	East 2nd Street	Elmer C. Strong	Shipping Clerk- Dept. Store
5	East 2nd Street	James Barnett	Manager & Deputy- Dept. Store

5	East 2nd Street	Elsie Barnett	
8	East 2nd Street	Josiah F. James	
10	East 2nd Street	Charles Boyd	Telephone Manager- YMCA
11	East 2nd Street	Leroy W. Tucker	
11	East 2nd Street	Mary Tucker	School Teacher
12	East 2nd Street	Robert Ewing	
13	East 2nd Street	Thomas Cole	Salesman- Dept. Store
14	East 2nd Street	Wilson M. Brown	
15	East 2nd Street	Burke Powell	Physician
16	East 2nd Street	Edward A. Carter	Physician
16	East 2nd Street	James Warren	Office Boy- Doctor Office
19	East 2nd Street	Adrien Longlois	Show- Theater
19	East 2nd Street	Hellen Longlois	Show- Theater
20	East 2nd Street	Charles Mease	
20	East 2nd Street	Edward Mease	Newsboy
20	East 2nd Street	Leo Mease	Newsboy
21	East 2nd Street	Albert Anderson	
23	East 2nd Street	Lewis Weaver	
23	East 2nd Street	Henry Weaver	Manager- Barn
23	East 2nd Street	Rosa Bush	
25	East 2nd Street	Elmer Anderson	
26	East 2nd Street	Thorton A. Coleman	
27	East 2nd Street	William Mattheson	Tailor
28	East 2nd Street	Sarah Shelton	Boardinghouse
28	East 2nd Street	Thomas Brown	
28	East 2nd Street	Minnie Brown	
28	East 2nd Street	Richard Douglas	
28	East 2nd Street	Robert Blakey	
29	East 2nd Street	Walter R. Woods	
31	East 2nd Street	Thomas W. Gowdy	Teamster- Dept. Store
31	East 2nd Street	David Bell	
32	East 2nd Street	James H. L. Neal	
33	East 2nd Street	James Compton	
33	East 2nd Street	Etheal Thomas	
34	East 2nd Street	Ben Tate	Carpenter
34	East 2nd Street	William Tate	
33	East 2nd Street	Oliver Ampy	
37	East 2nd Street	George Mason	
38	East 2nd Street	Richard W. March	Machine Shop
40	East 2nd Street	Walter Griffin	Laborer- Machine Shop
41	East 2nd Street	Ida M. Clair	
42	East 2nd Street	Samuel McKalvie	
44	East 2nd Street	Henry Sandridge	

LeeAnn Dickey

No.	Street	Name	Occupation
1	West 2nd Street	Albert Peterson	Salesman- Dept. Store
2	West 2nd Street	Lewis M. Edwards	Mechanic- Machine Shop
3	West 2nd Street	James M. Prentice	Blacksmith- Company Shop
3	West 2nd Street	Bessie Prentice	School Teacher
3	West 2nd Street	Marie A. Porter	
4	West 2nd Street	William Pierce	Deputy Sheriff
4	West 2nd Street	Lula Bishop	
5	West 2nd Street	John F. Landine	Salesman- Shoe Store
5	West 2nd Street	Mary E. Smith	Clerk- Store Office
7	West 2nd Street	Jessie M. Sears	
8	West 2nd Street	Herndon Reasby	
9	West 2nd Street	Carl Johnson	
9	West 2nd Street	Dave Johnson	
11	West 2nd Street	James Walker	
12	West 2nd Street	William P. Lewis	Salesman- Hardware Store
1	West 1st Street	Salon C. Welch	Undertaker- Depot House
4	West 1st Street	Paulina Burns	
4	West 1st Street	Lucy Mealy	Midwife
4	West 1st Street	Allan White	
4	West 1st Street	Lula Willis	
4	West 1st Street	George Willis	
4	West 1st Street	Dock Prentice	
6	West 1st Street	Frank W. Phillips	Salesman- Dept. Store
7	West 1st Street	Frank W. Hyatt	Salesman- Dept. Store
8	West 1st Street	Harry C. Austin	Engineer- Coal Mine
9	West 1st Street	Roscoe D. Buckingham	Salesman- Dept. Store
10	West 1st Street	Peter Larson	
11	West 1st Street	Miles Caurten	Station Agent- Railroad
12	West 1st Street	Frank A. Kent	Salesman- Dry Goods Store
14	West 1st Street	William Garnett	
14	West 1st Street	John Anderson	
1	East 1st Street	Ariel S. Dempsey	Electrician- Coal Company
2	East 1st Street	Mart Welch	Salesman- Dept. Store
5	East 1st Street	Marsh Erb	Salesman- Dept. Store
5	East 1st Street	Flossie Hale	Salesman- Dept. Store
8	East 1st Street	James Sheperd	
8	East 1st Street	Walker Reasby	
9	East 1st Street	George Child	Clerk- Office
9	East 1st Street	Maude Child	Office Girl- Telephone
9	East 1st Street	Pearl Child	Sales- Dept. Store
10	East 1st Street	Louisa Greaver	
10	East 1st Street	Lizzie Watkins	
10	East 1st Street	Maggie Watkins	
10	East 1st Street	Jones Watkins	

10	East 1st Street	Robert Boles	
10	East 1st Street	Henry Boles	
12	East 1st Street	William W. Lee	Mechanic- Machine Shop
11	East 1st Street	Jack Wynn	Foreman- Barn
11	East 1st Street	Earl Phipps	Laborer- Machine Shop
11	East 1st Street	Dan Cassidy	Carpenter
13	East 1st Street	James Chambers	
13	East 1st Street	Clyde E. Williams	
14	East 1st Street	Elias E. Clifton	Engineer- Electrician
15	East 1st Street	Edward Johnson	
15	East 1st Street	Charley Wilson	Barber
16	East 1st Street	Orville Barnett	Tester- Company Store
16	East 1st Street	Leota Bucklie	
17	East 1st Street	Elmer May	Teamster- Company Store
18	East 1st Street	Evans Reese	
19	East 1st Street	Richard Stewart	Supt. Bldg.-YMCA
20	East 1st Street	John B. Lewis	
20	East 1st Street	Thomas Williams	
21	East 1st Street	Albert Jordon	Night Watch Man- Store
21	East 1st Street	Fred Jordon	Teamster- Company Store
21	East 1st Street	Edna Jordon	Sales- Dept. Store
21	East 1st Street	Leo Lewis	Carpenter
22	East 1st Street	Lewis Leiby	
22	East 1st Street	Viola Garland	
22	East 1st Street	Charley Garland	
23	East 1st Street	Charles A. Hjort	
23	East 1st Street	Ernest Price	
24	East 1st Street	George Mordue	
24	East 1st Street	Annie Goldsberry	
24	East 1st Street	Francis Hocking	
25	East 1st Street	Henry Wilson	
27	East 1st Street	George M. Miller	
28	East 1st Street	James Blair	
28	East 1st Street	Roy Chambers	
28	East 1st Street	Mattie Chambers	Sales- Company Store
28	East 1st Street	Ethel Chambers	
28	East 1st Street	Willie Chambers	
28	East 1st Street	James Chambers	
29	East 1st Street	Marvin D. Cox	Minister- Pastor
2	A Street	Arthur Balls	
2	A Street	John Fish	
2	A Street	Robert G. Potter	
2	A Street	Alonzo Potter	
5	A Street	Roy A. Babcock	Master Mechanic
6	A Street	Sam Daniels	

LeeAnn Dickey

6	A Street	Florence Fay	
7	A Street	Delmar Snodgrass	Mechanic- Machine Shop
8	A Street	Charles L. Blackstone	Electrician- Shops
10	A Street	James Wynn	Machinist- Coal Shoots
12	A Street	James Smith	Engineering- Coal Mines
12	A Street	Clarence Chatman	Engineering- Coal Mines
13	A Street	Harvey W. Thomas	
14	A Street	John H. Masters	Foreman- Mine Labor
14	A Street	Marcia H. Masters	Office Girl- Telephones
15	A Street	Evan P. Thomas	
15	A Street	Nina M. Thomas	Booker- Grocery Store
16	A Street	Robert R. Amber	Contractor- Builder
18	A Street	William Vance	
19	A Street	Lewis Theurer	
19	A Street	Matilda Stone	Boardinghouse
19	A Street	Elsie Stone	
19	A Street	Hector McLean	
19	A Street	Charley Bortugal	Foreman- Coal Mines
21	A Street	Morgan G. Gardner	
22	A Street	Andrew Carlson	Blacksmith- Company Shop
22	A Street	Chester Nelson	
22	A Street	Hellen Nelson	
3	B Street	Charles E. Clair	
2	B Street	Otto Gustesson	Salesman- Dept. Store
1	B Street	John Green	
1	B Street	Emery Green	Teamster- Grocery Store
0	B Street	Natalie Franklin	
0	B Street	Gust Carlson	
	East Swede Town	Otto Bengtson	Miner
	East Swede Town	Oscar Peterson	Miner
	East Swede Town	Mary Carlbert	
	East Swede Town	Ellen Carlbert	Dressmaker
	East Swede Town	Frank L. Hyde	Carpenter
	East Swede Town	Victor O. Peterson	Miner
	East Swede Town	Carolina Leaf	
	East Swede Town	Oscar Johnson	Laborer
	East Swede Town	Carl Sylven	Miner
	East Swede Town	Algot Carlson	Laborer
	East Swede Town	Carl J. Peterson	Miner
	East Swede Town	John Anderson	Miner
	East Swede Town	Mary Olson	
	East Swede Town	John A. Nelson	Miner
	East Swede Town	Alma N. Nelson	Cook- Hospital

East Swede Town	Robert Nelson	Sales- Grocery
East Swede Town	Greta Johnson	
East Swede Town	Emil Johnson	Miner
East Swede Town	Anna L. Peterson	
East Swede Town	Carl F. Peterson	Sales- Grocery
East Swede Town	Albin Anderson	Miner
East Swede Town	Bernard Parker	
East Swede Town	Anna Parker	
East Swede Town	Wilson Jones	Miner
East Swede Town	Stella Richey	
East Swede Town	Aralia Richey	
East Swede Town	Estella Richey	
East Swede Town	Willie W. Jones	Miner
East Swede Town	Charles O. Carlson	Miner
East Swede Town	Oscar Almquist	Miner
East Swede Town	Charles A. Bloom	Miner
East Swede Town	John P. Swanson	Miner
East Swede Town	Charles G. Erickson	Miner
East Swede Town	Hans A. Carlson	
East Swede Town	Richard Olson	Miner
East Swede Town	Oscar Olson	Miner
East Swede Town	August Konash	Miner
East Swede Town	Joe Martenisko	Miner
East Swede Town	Mike Sivak	Miner
East Swede Town	Theodor Matussin	
East Swede Town	James A. Page	Miner
East Swede Town	Rosa A. McRoberts	Sales- Dept. Store
Armstrong's Section	Carrie L. Brown	
Armstrong's Section	Edward Barrett	Butcher- Shop
Armstrong's Section	William Goldsmith	Butcher- Market
Armstrong's Section	Frank Bridges	Butcher
Armstrong's Section	Carl J. Johnson	Miner
Armstrong's Section	Sarah Johnson	Washerwoman
Armstrong's Section	Birtha Jackson	Waiter- Restaurant
Armstrong's Section	Martha Callaway	Servant- Private Family
Armstrong's Section	Arian Jones	
West Swede Town	John F. Larson	Miner
West Swede Town	Charles Iaacson	Miner
West Swede Town	Mable J. Iaacson	Salesgirl- Dept. Store
West Swede Town	Sam Olson	
West Swede Town	Henry Holm	Miner
West Swede Town	Charles Cruise	Miner
West Swede Town	Wilhemia Cruise	Nurse- Private Family
West Swede Town	Alex Cruise	Sales- Dept. Store

LeeAnn Dickey

West Swede Town	Ruth Cruise	Sales- Dept. Store
West Swede Town	Judith Cruise	Cashier- Dept. Store
West Swede Town	Hilma Swanson	
West Swede Town	Sanford Had	Laborer- Coal Mine
West Swede Town	Lars J. Larson	Miner
West Swede Town	Charley Troselius	Miner
West Swede Town	Hilba Troselius	Bookkeeper- Co. Store
West Swede Town	Hugo Troselius	Sales- Dept. Store
West Swede Town	John Cadell	
West Swede Town	Victor Gustvson	Miner
West Swede Town	John Larson	Miner
West Swede Town	Gertie Anderson	
West Swede Town	Peter Peterson	Miner
West Swede Town	Alfred Peterson	Miner
West Swede Town	Henry Nicholas	Miner
West Swede Town	Madison Yancy	Miner
West Swede Town	Hobart White	Miner
West Swede Town	Charles Watson	Deputy Sheriff
West Swede Town	Goldia Thomas	Miner
West Swede Town	Mary Bedford	
West Swede Town	Colonel Y. Tolson	Miner
West Swede Town	William S. Bryson	Miner
West Swede Town	Gust Engstrom	Miner
West Swede Town	Charles Fisher	Miner
West Swede Town	Howard Ashby	Miner
West Swede Town	Lizzie Ashby	Farm Laborer
West Swede Town	Henry Burkett	Miner
West Swede Town	Maggie Burkett	Farm Laborer
West Swede Town	John Jenkins	Farmer
West Swede Town	Hester Jenkins	
West Swede Town	Sam Jenkins	Miner
West Swede Town	William London	Furniture Store Merchant
West Swede Town	Minnie London	School Teacher
West Swede Town	Hubert London	Deliveryman
West Swede Town	Will B. Rhodes	Miner
West Swede Town	Mary Rhodes	Keeper- Grocery Store
West Swede Town	John Harvey	Farmer
West Swede Town	Sherman Baker	Miner
West Swede Town	John C. Smith	Miner
West Swede Town	Lennie Golighty	
West Swede Town	Hazel Golighty	
West Swede Town	William J. Jones	Carpenter
West Swede Town	Bennie Jones	Carpenter
West Swede Town	Charley Jones	Miner
West Swede Town	Edward Jones	Carpenter
West Swede Town	James Richardson	Miner
West Swede Town	Robert J. Walker	Miner

West Swede Town	Charles Rice	Miner
West Swede Town	Armsted Fortune	Laborer- Coal Mine
West Swede Town	Robert Stone	Laborer- Coal Mine
West Swede Town	George G. Williams	Miner
West Swede Town	Amanda Esshom	
West Swede Town	Edward R. Esshom	Salesman- Dept. Store
West Swede Town	Sam Rhodes	Miner
West Swede Town	Mary Chatman	
West Swede Town	Early Blackman	Miner
West Swede Town	Reaner Blackman	Washerwoman
West Swede Town	George Brown	Miner
West Swede Town	Newton Cross	Miner
West Swede Town	Charles G. Southall	Mason- Brick
West Swede Town	Julia Southall	Dressmaker
West Swede Town	Charles Reeser	Mechanic- Machine Shop
West Swede Town	Carl Carlson	Mechanic- Machine Shop
West Swede Town	Gust Guillman	Miner
West Swede Town	Arthur L. Tennant	Bookkeeper- Company Office
West Swede Town	James Watson	Miner
West Swede Town	Jennet Watson	Salesgirl- Dept. Store
West Swede Town	Edward Brown	Miner
West Swede Town	Salmon Shelton	Miner
West Swede Town	Stella Davis	
West Swede Town	Richard Shelton	Miner
West Swede Town	Arthur Mickens	Miner
West Swede Town	John Cooper	Miner
West Swede Town	Henry Russel	Miner
West Swede Town	Golda Taylor	Laborer- General
West Swede Town	Sloan Taylor	Miner
West Swede Town	Margaret Kooker	
West Swede Town	Herman Kooker	Driver- Coal Mine
West Swede Town	Edith Harris	
West Swede Town	Roy Holdsworth	Cook- Bakery
West Swede Town	Isabella Knight	
West Swede Town	Lee Devorst	Miner
West Swede Town	Andrew Adams	Miner
West Swede Town	John H. Whitler	Miner
West Swede Town	John Sander	Miner
West Swede Town	Charles E. Hartman	Miner
West Swede Town	James L. Cooper	Laborer- Coal Mine
West Swede Town	Frances Cooper	
West Swede Town	Joseph Roman	Miner
West Swede Town	Nathaniel McDowell	Miner
West Swede Town	Frank Price	Miner
West Swede Town	George Kitsmiller	
West Swede Town	David Peterson	Salesman- Grocery
West Swede Town	John Peterson	

LeeAnn Dickey

West Swede Town	Clark M. Paris	
West Swede Town	Clark Paris Jr.	Mechanic- Machine Shop
West Swede Town	Paris	Newsboy
West Swede Town	Alfred E. Thomas	Druggist
West Swede Town	Anna Chambers	
West Swede Town	Constance Chambers	
West Swede Town	Andrew Jeffers	Keeper- Restaurant
West Swede Town	Matilda Williams	Cook- Restaurant
West Swede Town	Claude McBride	
West Swede Town	George E. Calloway	Salesman- Tailor
West Swede Town	Walter Ward	
West Swede Town	Jessie Reed	
West Swede Town	Daniel E. Butler	Minister- Pastor
West Swede Town	James W. Goings	Barber- Own Shop
West Swede Town	Sarah Williams	
West Swede Town	Isaac J. Cobbs	Supt. Coal Company
West Swede Town	Phillip Cobbs	Prospecting- Driller
West Swede Town	William Cobbs	Prospecting- Driller
West Swede Town	John Baxter	Butcher- Own Shop
West Swede Town	Lottie Baxter	Cashier- Bank
West Swede Town	Hobart A. Armstrong	Butcher- Market
West Swede Town	Carelton E. Cliff	Sales- Dry Goods Store
West Swede Town	Emma T. Christy	Manager- Company Office
West Swede Town	Nellie Evans	Bookkeeper- Dept. Store
West Swede Town	William L. Perkins	Keeper- Hotel
West Swede Town	Rebecca Perkins	Keeper- Hotel
West Swede Town	Mary Perkins	Hair Dresser
West Swede Town	Willa Perkins	Asst. Manager- Hotel
West Swede Town	Thomas Perkins	
West Swede Town	Robert A. Perkins	Keeper- Hotel
West Swede Town	Arthur M. Fletcher	Barber- Own Shop
West Swede Town	Eugene Lee	Barber Shop
West Swede Town	John Williams	Keeper- Restaurant
West Swede Town	Eric F. Brown	Cashier- Consolidated Coal Co.
West Swede Town	William A. Flynn	Clerk- Coal Office
West Swede Town	Clayton Ristine	Asst. Cashier- Coal Office
West Swede Town	Elmer Baysoar	Supt. Consolidated Coal
West Swede Town	Charles E. Allen	Janitor-YMCA
West Swede Town	Ethylle Abegglen	Clerk- Coal Offices
West Swede Town	LaBelle McNeeley	Saleswoman
West Swede Town	Anna Crowley	
West Swede Town	Frank S. Jorgensen	Engineering
West Swede Town	Herbert Brewer	Sales- Dept. Store
West Swede Town	Roy R. McRae	
West Swede Town	Lavinia S. Hammond	
West Swede Town	Briscoe Miller	
West Swede Town	Sam Cleveland	

West Swede Town	Archie Madison	
West Swede Town	Eve Williams	Drayman- Streets
West Swede Town	Clyde Williams	Drayman- Streets
West Swede Town	John Bartow	Plumber- Steam pipe
West Swede Town	Fred H. Putnam	Baker- Bakery
West Swede Town	Charles W. Armstrong	Butcher
West Swede Town	John T. Roman	
West Swede Town	Mary J. Roman	
West Swede Town	George W. Walters	
West Swede Town	William P. Jackson	
West Swede Town	Leona Smith	
West Swede Town	Clayton R. Foster	
West Swede Town	Randolph Taylor	Engineer
West Swede Town	Ollie Woods	
West Swede Town	John H. Mosley	
West Swede Town	Edward Calvert	
West Swede Town	Allen Jones	Mechanic- Blacksmith
West Swede Town	Martha Wright	
West Swede Town	Lawyer Freeman	
West Swede Town	Clark Stewart	Engineer- Stationary
West Swede Town	Martin Jones	Fireman- Stationary
West Swede Town	Joseph T. Thomas	
West Swede Town	Thomas W. Mitchell	
West Swede Town	Ethel D. Mitchell	
West Swede Town	Roy Madison	
West Swede Town	Gertrude Dyser	
West Swede Town	Pearl Bryson	
West Swede Town	George Danniel	Drayman- Street
West Swede Town	Eugene Turner	
West Swede Town	William H. Thomas	
West Swede Town	Elizabeth Scales	
West Swede Town	William Johnson	
West Swede Town	Peter Abington	
West Swede Town	Clifford Wallace	
West Swede Town	William Flynn	
West Swede Town	John J. Jones	
West Swede Town	Edward Mays	
West Swede Town	Pomp Burges	
West Swede Town	Lucinda Abington	
West Swede Town	Iva M. Christian	
West Swede Town	Beacher Christian	
West Swede Town	Toney Logan	
West Swede Town	Robert V. Porter	
West Swede Town	George Morrison	
West Swede Town	Richard Blakey	
West Swede Town	Annie Glenn	
West Swede Town	Mable Dysart	

LeeAnn Dickey

	West Swede Town	William Edward	
	West Swede Town	Edmond Forsyth	
	West Swede Town	Ralph McBride	
	West Swede Town	Lula Monroe	
	West Swede Town	Virginia Wade	Waiter- Restaurant
	West Swede Town	Francis Wade	
	West Swede Town	Anton Kimburgen	
	West Swede Town	William H. Bailey	
	West Swede Town	Roberta M. Bailey	Deputy Post Master
	West Swede Town	Dwight Grandbery	Tailor- Own Shop
	West Swede Town	Orville Bryant	
	West Swede Town	Jessie Rivers	
	West Swede Town	Chester Dishman	Porter- Store
52/52	Bluff Creek Twp.	Elijah Edinburgh	
57/57	Bluff Creek twp.	Tony Oliphant	
57/57	Bluff Creek Twp.	Caroline Oliphant	
86/86	Bluff Creek Twp.	Peter Doyle	
162/166	Bluff Creek Twp.	Alfred Guy	
170/174	Bluff Creek Twp.	Willis Turner	
171/175	Bluff Creek Twp.	Richard Green	
171/175	Bluff Creek Twp.	Lillie Faidley	
171/175	Bluff Creek Twp.	Lula Faidley	
171/175	Bluff Creek Twp.	Mary Faidley	
174/178	Bluff Creek Twp.	Richard Mayo	
174/178	Bluff Creek Twp.	John Williams	
178/182	Bluff Creek Twp.	James Whitehead	
178/182	Bluff Creek Twp.	Mae Carter	
178/182	Bluff Creek Twp.	J.C. Robinson	
178/182	Bluff Creek Twp.	William Price	
178/182	Bluff Creek Twp.	William Anderson	
178/182	Bluff Creek Twp.	Sarah Williams	
183/187	Bluff Creek Twp.	Jacob F. Brown	
203/208	Bluff Creek Twp.	James Ellis	
203/208	Bluff Creek Twp.	Nellie Pondexter	
204/209	Bluff Creek Twp.	Thomas Glass	
211/216	Bluff Creek Twp.	Reese Pondexter	
235/241	Bluff Creek Twp.	H.A. Armstrong	
241/248	Bluff Creek Twp	James Fields	
241/248	Bluff Creek Twp.	Lucy Winston	
242/249	Bluff Creek Twp.	John Lucas	
243/250	Bluff Creek Twp.	W.M. Smith	
244/251	Bluff Creek Twp.	Emanuel	
244/251	Bluff Creek Twp.	Hattie	
245/252	Bluff Creek Twp.	Stephen Guy	
246/253	Bluff Creek Twp.	Edward Downs	

(Michael W. Lemberger)

246/253	Bluff Creek Twp.	Frank Brown
247/254	Bluff Creek Twp.	C.M. Walker
248/255	Bluff Creek Twp	William L. Reasby
249/256	Bluff Creek Twp.	J.E. Burks
253/260	Bluff Creek Twp.	Isaac Woodford
255/262	Bluff Creek Twp.	John W. Neely
255/252	Bluff Creek Twp.	Aline Sams
256/263	Bluff Creek Twp.	John Taylor
256/263	Bluff Creek Twp.	Edgar Harris
257/263	Bluff Creek Twp.	L.B. Handon
258/264	Bluff Creek Twp.	Isaac H. Hutchison
259/265	Bluff Creek Twp.	Robert Davis
259/265	Bluff Creek Twp.	Ethel Jackson
260/266	Bluff Creek Twp.	Robert Vohn
260/266	Bluff Creek Twp.	Edith Madison
260/266	Bluff Creek Twp.	Archie Madison
260/266	Bluff Creek Twp.	Dave Coeman
261/267	Bluff Creek Twp.	H.J. Williams
261/267	Bluff Creek Twp.	John Williams
261/267	Bluff Creek Twp.	William Wright
262/268	Bluff Creek Twp.	King Slaughter
262/268	Bluff Creek Twp.	Pearl Floyd
263/269	Bluff Creek Twp.	James Roper
264/270	Bluff Creek Twp.	Henry Giles
265/271	Bluff Creek Twp.	Henry Davis
266/272	Bluff Creek Twp.	Moletus Rhodes
267/272	Bluff Creek Twp.	P.A. Reeves
268/274	Bluff Creek Twp.	W.H. Reeves
270/276	Bluff Creek Twp.	James Devering
270/276	Bluff Creek Twp.	Mary Adkinson
270/276	Bluff Creek Twp.	Charlie Harvey
274/280	Bluff Creek Twp.	Samuel Simmons
274/280	Bluff Creek Twp	Jackson Garland
277/283	Bluff Creek Twp.	C.J. Lyons
283/289	Bluff Creek Twp.	Green Garrett
283/289	Bluff Creek Twp.	Leroy White
300/306	Bluff Creek Twp.	Ruth Stuele
300/306	Bluff Creek Twp.	West Wood
300/306	Bluff Creek Twp.	H.P. Goff
302/308	Bluff Creek Twp.	Grant Brown
309/315	Bluff Creek Twp.	M. Henderson
310/316	Bluff Creek Twp.	Sampson Johnson
310/316	Bluff Creek Twp.	William Reasby
310/316	Bluff Creek Twp.	Sidney Sanders
310/316	Bluff Creek Twp.	Josephine Woodford
311/317	Bluff Creek Twp.	John Blakey

312/318	Bluff Creek Twp.	Lucy Walker
312/318	Bluff Creek Twp.	Abraham Chappman
313/319	Bluff Creek Twp.	Minor Waites
344/351	Bluff Creek Twp.	Louis Nolan
344/351	Bluff Creek Twp.	Lee Nolan
345/352	Bluff Creek Twp.	William Humbles
346/353	Bluff Creek Twp.	J.H. Bates
347/354	Bluff Creek Twp.	Henry Harris
347/354	Bluff Creek Twp.	Sony Baker
348/355	Bluff Creek Twp.	James Qualls
349/356	Bluff Creek Twp.	John Chapman
350/357	Bluff Creek Twp.	W.H. Allen
356/363	Bluff Creek Twp.	William Tolen
356/363	Bluff Creek Twp	Florence Graves
356/363	Bluff Creek Twp	William Graves
356/363	Bluff Creek Twp.	Anna L. Graves
359/366	Bluff Creek Twp.	William Early

Consolidation Coal Company pay day -- July 4, 1907. (Monroe County Historical Museum.)

Buxton Death Records

Information in this list has been assembled from death records in Monroe County and Mahaska County, Iowa, on the burials at Buxton Cemetery. Where available, the parents' names and their birth state are listed. Listing is not alphabetical.

A:

Arthur, Sally May
Died: July 8, 1907 Aged: 2y 6d Born: July 2, 1905 in Iowa Buried: July 9, 1907
Father: Geo. W. Arthur (VA) Mother: Sally Tanks
Anderson, Roma
Died: June 19, 1909 Aged: 4y 11m 9d Born: January 1, 1905 in Iowa Buried: June 21, 1909
Father: Frank Anderson (TN) Mother: Lulu Chapman
Ampey, Dorothy M. (Book 2A Page 33 Monroe County)
Died: December 1, 1906 Aged: 3y 10d Born: February 1, 1903 in Iowa Buried: December 3, 1906
Father: John Ampey (VA) Mother: Louisa Harris
Allen, Unnamed (Book 2A Page 47 Monroe County)
Died: February 13, 1907 Aged: 78y Born: Illinois Buried: February 15, 1907
Father: Unnamed Mother: Unnamed
Allen, Unnamed (Book 2A Page 104 Monroe County)
Died: December 5, 1907 No Age Given Born: Iowa Buried: December 6, 1907
Father: Baxter Allen (NC) Mother: Mattie Glenn
Allen, Baby (Book 2A Page 185 Monroe County)
Died: April 27, 1909 Aged: 27d Born: March 20, 1909 in Iowa Buried: April 29, 1909
Father: Unnamed Mother: Jessie Allen
Abington, Jane (Book 2B Page 101 Monroe County)
Died: March 2, 1916 Aged: 40y 3m 1d Born: December 1, 1875 in Ohio Buried: March 6, 1916
Father: Andrew Jackson Mother: Sallie Prosser Status: Married
Anderson, Gertrude (Book 2A Page 11 Monroe County)
Died: September 14, 1906 Aged: 6m 26d Born: February 19, 1906 in Illinois Buried: September 17, 1906
Father: Herbert Anderson (IL) Mother: Gertrude Pondexster
Allen, John Henry (Book 2A Page 468 Monroe County)
Died: June 19, 1914 Aged: 59y Born: March in Virginia Buried: June 21, 1914
Father: Martin Allen (VA) Mother: Judith Brown

B:

Blakey, Georgia Alice (Book 1 1897- 1935 Monroe County)
Died: May 25, 1903 Aged: 3y 11m 23d Born: Muchakinock, Iowa Buried: No Date Given
No Parents' Names Listed

Burkey, John Henry (Book 1 1897- 1935 Monroe County)
Died: December 23, 1903 Aged: 8y 3m Born: Carbondale, Iowa Buried: No Date Given
No Parents' Names Listed

Bowles, Alice (Book 2A Page 6 Monroe County)
Died: August 31, 1906 Aged: 35y 6m 15d Born: March 15, 1871 in Virginia Buried: September 2, 1906
Father: Sam'l Watkins (VA) Mother: Louise Douglas

Baird, Stella E. (Book 2A Page 11 Monroe County)
Died: September 21, 1906 Aged: 9y 1m 22d Born: July 30, 1897 in Iowa Buried: September 24, 1906
Father: Sep Baird (IL) Mother: Eliz. James

Burkett, Unnamed (Book 2A Page 12 Monroe County)
Died: September 25, 1906 No Age Given Born: Sept. 1906 Buried: September 25, 1906
Father: George Burkett Mother: Mrs. Burkett

Blainey, Molly (Book 2A Page 19 Monroe County)
Died: October 3, 1906 Aged: 18y 2m 14d Born: July 15, 1888 in Virginia Buried: October 4, 1906
Father: J.R. Blainey (VA) Mother: Laura V. Gibson

Brown, Electra (Book 2A Page 27 Monroe County)
Died: November 15, 1906 Aged: 18y 8m 7d Born: February 28, 1889 in Iowa Buried: November 15, 1906
Father: R.J. Brown (VA) Mother: Ida Brown

Berges, Howard (Book 2A Page 39 Monroe County)
Died: January 13, 1907 Aged: 27y Born: July 4, 1879 in North Carolina Buried: January 16, 1907
Father: Unnamed Mother: Unnamed Status: Married

Boston, Wm. M. (Book 2A Page 39 Monroe County)
Died: January 9, 1907 Aged: 7m 8d Born: May 31, 1906 in Iowa Buried: January 11, 1907
Father: Unnamed Mother: Minnie Boston

Funeral procession in Buxton. (Monroe County Historical Museum.)

Boston, William (1906- 1911 Mahaska County)
Died: September 24, 1910 Aged: Not Given Born: September 24, 1883 in Maryland
Buried: Not Given Father: Not Given Mother: Not Given
Bowers, Joe (Book 2A Page 39 Monroe County)
Died: January 22, 1907 Aged: 20y 10m 1d Born: March 22, 1880 in North Carolina Buried: January 25, 1907
Father: Joe Bowers (NC) Mother: Unnamed
Burgess, Roxie (Book 2A Page 48 Monroe County)
Died: February 23, 1907 Aged: 24y 6m 18d Born: September 5, 1883 in Virginia Buried: February 25, 1907
Father: Pomp Burgess (VA) Mother: Minta
Baker, Kittie (Book 2A Page 54 Monroe County)
Died: March 16, 1907 Aged: 82y Born: Virginia Buried: March 18, 1907
Father: Granger Watts Mother: Unnamed Status: Married
Burgess, Minta (Book 2A Page 75 Monroe County)
Died: June 29, 1907 Aged: 59y 3m Born: March 1849 in Virginia Buried: June 30, 1907
Father: Unnamed Joice Mother: Nellie Joice Status: Married
Barbee, Unnamed (Book 2A Page 101 Monroe County)
Died: November 15, 1907 Stillborn Born: November 15, 1907 in Iowa Buried: November 16, 1907
Father: Leonard Barbee (TN) Mother: Mattie Offercer
Baker, Marie C. (Book 2A Page 105 Monroe County)
Died: December 30, 1907 Aged: 9m 12d Born: March 18, 1906 in Iowa Buried: January 1, 1908
Father: John Baker (NC) Mother: Minnie Fields
Braxton, Cora E. (Book 2A Page 132 Monroe County)
Died: May 11, 1908 Aged: 18y Born: Virginia Buried: May 14, 1908 Buried: May 14, 1908
Father: Unnamed Mother: Unnamed
Banner, Mattie (Book 2A Page 154 Monroe County)
Died: November 1, 1908 No Age Given Born: August 10, 1856 in Virginia Buried: November 2, 1908
Father: Sam Calmer (VA) Mother: Unnamed Status: Married
Blainey, Ardell J. (Book 2A Page 155 Monroe County, Iowa)
Died: November 6, 1908 Aged: 28d Born: October 13, 1908 in Iowa Buried: November 7, 1908
Father: Walter Blainey (VA) Mother: C. Crushshon
Bryant, Hannah (Book 2A Page 155 Monroe County)
Died: November 15, 1908 Aged: 73y Born: Virginia Buried: November 18, 1908
Father: Sam Cole (VA) Mother: Unnamed Status: Widowed
Bennett, Zelma Marie (Book 2A Page 186 Monroe County)
Died: April 25, 1909 Aged: 7m 6d Born: September 19, 1908 in Iowa Buried: April 27, 1909
Father: Ace Bennett (AL) Mother: Lucy Carry
Bryson, Maggie (Book 2A Page 234 Monroe County)
Died: January 31, 1911 Aged: 35y 10m 1d Born: April 4 in Virginia Buried: February 2, 1911
Father: William Rolland Mother: Unknown Status: Married
Booker, Herman (Book 2A Page 263 Monroe County)
Died: June 27, 1911 Aged: 1y 3m 12d Born: March 15, 1910 in Iowa Buried: June 28, 1911
Father: R.A. Booker (VA) Mother: Emma Robinson
Blainey, Mrs. Laura V. (Book 2A Page 319 Monroe County)
Died: March 4, 1912 Aged: 58y 10m Born: May 4, 1854 in Virginia Buried: March 7, 1912
Father: Unnamed Gibson (VA) Mother: Unknown Status: Married

Booker, Eliza (Book 2A Page 319 Monroe County)
Died: March 18, 1912 Aged: abt 62y Born: Virginia Buried: March 21, 1912
Father: David Woodson (VA) Mother: Unknown Status: Married
Baker, King (Book 2A Page 349 Monroe County)
Died: September 8, 1912 Aged: abt 68y Born: Virginia Buried: September 9, 1912
Father: Unnamed Mother: Unnamed Status: Single
Bates, Henry Clifford (Book 2A Page 349 Monroe County)
Died: September 28, 1912 Aged: 23y 9m 12d Born: December 16, 1888 in Iowa Buried: October 1, 1912
Father: J.H. Bates (VA) Mother: Marietta Sims
Blackman, Rena (Book 2A Page 361 Monroe County)
Died: December 29, 1912 Aged: abt 57y Born: Virginia Buried: June 1, 1913
Father: Unnamed Mayo Mother: Mary Deans Status: Married
Brinker, Bengiman Ernest (Book 2A Page 402 Monroe County)
Died: July 30, 1913 Aged: 2y 3m 23d Born: April 2, 1911 in Illinois Buried: August 2, 1913
Father: Ray Brinker (MO) Mother: Daisy Anderson
Baker, Simmon (Book 2A Page 411 Monroe County)
Died: August 27, 1913 Aged: 91y Born: Virginia Buried: August 29, 1913
Father: Unnamed Mother: Unnamed Informant: Henry Harris Status: Widowed
Brown, Malcenia (Book 2A Page 420 Monroe County)
Died: October 13, 1913 Aged: 9m 2d Born: January 10, 1912 in Iowa Buried: October 14, 1913
Father: Unknown Mother: Grace Brown
Buttram, Landon (Book 2A Page 462 Monroe County)
Died: May 8, 1914 Aged: 13y 11m 19d Born: May 27, 1901 in Tennessee Buried: May 10, 1914
Father: George Buttram (TN) Mother: Mattie McKee
Byers, Loyd (Book 2A Page 462 Monroe County)
Died: May 21, 1914 Aged: 26y 2m 16d Born: September 5, 1888 in Iowa Buried: May 23, 1914
Father: James Byers (VA) Mother: Emma Lewis Status: Single
Brooks, James (Book 2B Page 1 Monroe County)
Died: July 30, 1914 Aged: 13y 3m 25d Born: April 5, 1901 in Iowa Buried: August 1, 1914
Father: Wm. Brooks (VA) Mother: Sallie Harrell Status: Single
Butram, Loyd (Book 2B Page 1 Monroe County)
Died: July 28, 1914 Aged: 8y 0m 26d Born: September 2, 1905 in Iowa Buried: August 1, 1914
Father: George Butram (TN) Mother: Mattie McKee
Brooks, Annie Elisabeth (Book 2B Page 5 Monroe County)
Died: August 5, 1914 Aged: 9y 4m 24d Born: March 12, 1905 in Iowa Buried: August 6, 1914
Father: Wm. Brooks (VA) Mother: Sallie Harrell
Bryson, Carl (Book 2B Page 5 Monroe County)
Died: August 10, 1914 Aged: 13y 6m 4d Born: February 6, 1901 in Illinois Buried: August 12, 1914
Father: Wm. S. Bryson (NC) Mother: Maggie White
Beadle, Charles (Book 2B Page 30 Monroe County)
Died: February 24, 1915 Aged: 43y 11m 20d Born: Virginia Buried: February 26, 1915
Father: Unknown Mother: Unknown Status: Single
Bates, Essie May (Book 2B Page 31 Monroe County)
Died: February 21, 1915 Aged: 19y 9m 4d Born: May 17 Buried: February 25, 1915
Father: C.H. Watson (VA) Mother: Francis Bedford Status: Married

Brown, Mary (Book 2B Page 115 Monroe County)
Died: May 20, 1916 Aged: 47y 4m 3d Born: January 17, 1869 in Virginia Buried: May 22, 1916
Father: Rufus Blainer (VA) Mother: Feebie Taylor Informant: Wesley Allen Status: Married
Bolden, Bert (Book 2B Page 146 Monroe County)
Died: November 24, 1916 Aged: 10y 7m 26d Born: March 28, 1906 in Iowa Buried: November 25, 1916
Father: Lee Bolden (VA) Mother: Maude Hams
Baldress, Florance (Book 2B Page 176 Monroe County)
Died: May 9, 1917 Stillborn Born: May 9, 1917 Buried: May 10, 1917
Father: Lee Baldress (VA) Mother: Mallia Harms
Bergstrom, Katrina (Book 2B Page 185 Monroe County)
Died: August 16, 1917 Aged: 81y 7m 1d Born: January 15, 1836 in Sweden Buried: August 19, 1917
Father: Bengt Johanson (Sweden) Mother: Bolla Anderson Status: Widowed
Brooks, George W. (Book 2B Page 196 Monroe County)
Died: October 11, 1917 Aged: 47y 5m 18d Born: April 23, 1870 in Virginia Buried: October 16, 1917
Father: George Brooks (VA) Mother: Peggie Rudd Status: Married
Bingham, Rebecca (Book 2B Page 230 Monroe County)
Died: April 2, 1918 Aged: 53y 3m 11d Born: December 22, 1864 in Virginia Buried: April 5, 1918
Father: Rush Henderson (VA) Mother: Unknown Status: Married
Brown, Hattie (Book 2B Page 257 Monroe County)
Died: August 17, 1918 Aged: 49y 12d Born: August 5, 1869 in Virginia Buried: August 21, 1918
Father: Rev. W.W. Williams (MO) Mother: Emma Woods (KY) Status: Married
Bates, Robert Douglas Book 2B Page 293 Monroe County)
Died: December 4, 1918 Aged: 99y 4m 17d Born: July 18, 1819 in Virginia Buried: December 7, 1918
Father: Rob't Douglas Bates Mother: Unknown Informant: Mrs. J.M. Simpson
Brown, John (Book 2B Page 91 Monroe County)
Died: September 18, 1907 Aged: 29y Born: Virginia Buried: September 23, 1907
Father: William Brown (VA) Mother: Martha Cox Status: Single
Barber, Bertha (June 1915- June 1919 Mahaska County)
Died: March 12, 1917 Aged: Not Given Born: December 19, 1892
Buried: Not Given Father: Not Given Mother: Not Given
Baker, Minnie Fields (June 1915- June 1919 Mahaska County)
Died: June 12, 1919 Aged: Not Given Born: September 18, 1873 in Missouri
Buried: Not Given Father: Not Given Mother: Not Given

C:

Cannady, John T. (Book 1 1897-1935 Monroe County)
Died: July 29, 1907 Aged: 54y 6m 29d Born: January 31, 1853 in Virginia Buried: July 31, 1907
Father: Creed Cannady (VA) Mother: Emeline Davis
Conwell, Mandy (Book 2A Page 1 Monroe County)
Died: July 23, 1906 Aged: abt 40y Born: Alabama Buried: July 25, 1906
Father: Unknown McDown (AL) Mother: Harriatt Sanders Status: Widowed
Cunningham, Unnamed (Book 2A Page 12 Monroe County)
Died: September 1, 1906 Aged: 3d Born: August 30, 1906 in Iowa Buried: September 2, 1906
Father: H.C. Cunningham (VA) Mother: Clara Hencock

Cunningham, Mrs. Clarence (Clara) (Book 2A Page 12 Monroe County)
Died: September 14, 1906 Aged: 35y Born: Virginia Buried: September 19, 1906
Father: Sam Handcock Mother: Unnamed Craggatt Status: Married
Cook, Eliz (Book 2A Page 28 Monroe County)
Died: November 1, 1906 Aged: 17y Born: April 8, 1889 in Alabama
Father: Troy Cook (VA) Mother: Emeline Epsen Status: Single
Carell, Henry (Book 2A Page 55 Monroe County)
Died: March 13, 1907 Aged: 18y Born: December 10 in Virginia Buried: March 16, 1907
Father: Rob't Carell (VA) Mother: Sarah Brown Status: Single
Carter, S.J. (Book 2A Page 75 Monroe County)
Died: June 30, 1907 Aged: 46y 11m Born: July 30, 1861 in Alabama Buried: July 2, 1907
Father: Mike Carter (SC) Mother: Unnamed Status: Married
Clinton, James C. (Book 2A Page 87 Monroe County)
Died: August 20, 1907 Aged: 1y 1m 20d Born: June 28, 1906 in Virginia Buried: August 20, 1907
Father: W.J. Clinton (SC) Mother: Alice Eaves
Coleman, Delia E. (Book 2A Page 161 Monroe County)
Died: December 3, 1908 Aged: 39y 16d Born: November 17, 1869 in Kentucky
Buried: December 6, 1908 Father: Anderson Baker (KY) Mother: Susan
Carrey, Bettie (Book 2A Page 213 Monroe County0
Died: September 11, 1910 Aged: 50y Born: Virginia Buried: September 19, 1910
Father: Unnamed Mother: Unnamed
Carpenter, Mildred A. (Book 2A Page 225 Monroe County)
Died: November 29, 1910 Aged: 44y 1m 21d Born: Virginia
Father: Archie Holland (VA) Mother: Unknown Status: Married
Compostine, Infant (Book 2A Page 225 Monroe County)
Died: November 25, 1910 Stillborn Born: November 25, 1910 Buried: November 25, 1910
Father: A. Compostine (Austria) Mother: Unnamed
Cross, Charlie H. (Book 2A Page 240 Monroe County)
Died: February 14, 1911 Aged: 59y Born: Virginia Buried: February 19, 1911
Father: Unnamed Mother: Unnamed
Croft, Infant (Book 2A Page 263 Monroe County)
Died: June 30, 1911 Stillborn Born: June 30, 1911 in Iowa Buried: July 1, 1911
Father: Ben Croft (IA) Mother: Etta Pierce
Cross, Augusta (Twin) (Book 2A Page 282 Monroe County)
Died: September 15, 1911 Aged: 1m 12d Born: August 6, 1911 Buried: September 16, 1911
Father: C.H. Cross (KY) Mother: Lizzy Lucas
Chatman, Mary Miller (Book 2A Page 286 Monroe County)
Died: October 26, 1911 Aged: 77y Born: Virginia Buried: October 28, 1911
Father: Unnamed Mother: Unnamed Status: Widowed
Compton, James (Book 2A Page 286 Monroe County)
Died: October 25, 1911 Aged: 40y Born: Virginia Buried: October 27, 1911
Father: Unnamed Mother: Unnamed Status: Married
Carr, Dorothy May (Book 2A Page 292 Monroe County)
Died: November 19, 1911 Aged: 5m 3d Born: July 16, 1911 in Iowa Buried: November 21, 1911
Father: George Carr (IA) Mother: Mary Robinson

Carrey, Mary F. (Book 2A Page 292 Monroe County)
Died: November 22, 1911 Aged: 32y 9m Born: February 1879 in Virginia
Buried: November 24, 1911 Father: John Blarney (VA) Mother: Mollie Gibson
Cobb, Robert (Book 2A Page 293 Monroe County)
Died: November 19, 1911 Aged: 54y Born: Virginia Buried: November 21, 1911
Father: Unnamed Cobb (VA) Mother: Unknown
Carter, Justeene (Book 2A Page 304 Monroe County)
Died: January 20, 1912 Aged: 22y 3m 20d Born: October 1, 1887 in Iowa Buried: January 23, 1912
Father: W.A. Carter (VA) Mother: Ellen Harris
Cross, August (Twin) (Book 2A Page 304 Monroe County)
Died: January 8, 1912 Aged: 4m Born: August 6, 1911 in Iowa Buried: January 9, 1912
Father: Charlie Cross (KY) Mother: Lizzy Slaughter
Cheatham, Eliza (Book 2A Page 312 Monroe County)
Died: February 19, 1912 Aged: 79y Born: Virginia Buried: February 22, 1912
Father: Jim Elliott (VA) Mother: Emana Elliott Status: Widowed
Crank, Mary S. (Book 2A Page 356 Monroe County)
Died: October 10, 1912 Aged: 44y Born: October 10, 1868 in Virginia Buried: October 13, 1912
Father: George D. Harris (VA) Mother: Susan Rebecca Berry
Carson, James (Book 2A Page 374 Monroe County)
Died: February 7, 1913 Aged: 38y Born: Tennessee Buried: February 10, 1913
Father: Unnamed Mother: Unnamed Status: Married
Carlson, Mrs. Anna D. (Book 2B Page 1 Monroe County)
Died: July 12, 1914 Aged: 79y Born: July 3, 1835 in Sweden Buried: July 14, 1914
Father: John Daniels (Sweden) Mother: Annie Sofie Daniels Status: Married
Carr, Mary (Book 2A Page 31 Monroe County)
Died: February 12, 1915 Aged: 38y 12d Born: February 1, 1877 in Virginia
Buried: February 15, 1915 Father: Unknown Mother: Unknown Status: Married
Carter, Chas. Nelson (Book 2A Page 31 Monroe County)
Died: February 16, 1915 Aged: 64y 4m 1d Born: October 15, 1850 in Virginia
Buried: February 18, 1915 Father: Unnamed Mother: Unnamed Status: Married
Chambers, Griffith (Book 2A Page38 Monroe County)
Died: March 3, 1915 Aged: 44y 1m 19d Born: January 12, 1871 in Virginia
Buried: March 4, 1915 Father: Unnamed Mother: Unnamed Status: Single
Carter, Jennie (Book 2B Page 53 Monroe County)
Died: June 17, 1915 Aged: 45y 3m Born: March 1870 in Virginia
Buried: June 21, 1915 Father: Unknown Mother: Elizabeth Wilkison Status: Married
Clark, Flossie (Book 2B Page 96 Monroe County)
Died: February 24, 1916 Aged: 5m 9d Born: September 15, 1915 in Iowa
Buried: February 26, 1916 Father: Unknown Mother: Danline Clark
Curtis, Priscilla (Book 2B Page 102 Monroe County)
Died: March 12, 1916 Aged: 58y Born: 1858 in Virginia Buried: March 15, 1916
Father: Unknown Mother: Unknown Status: Married
Carter, George Washington (Book 2B Page 230 Monroe County)
Died: April 19, 1918 Aged: 58y 7m Born: September 19, 1859 Buried: April 22, 1918
Father: Walter Carter (VA) Mother: Unnamed Status: Married

Crowder, Charles William (Book 2B Page269 Monroe County)
Died: October 4, 1918 Aged: 9y 9m 20d Born: February 14, 1909 in Enterprise, Iowa
Buried: October 4, 1918 Father: Linzie Crowder (VA) Mother: Rachel Clayborne
Carpenter, Winifred (Book 2B Page 319 Monroe County)
Died: March 1, 1919 Aged: 10d Born: February 19, 1919 in Buxton, Iowa
Buried: March 2, 1919 Father: Arclice Carpebter (VA) Mother: Mable Junkens (IA)
Carr, John M. (Book 2B Page 319 Monroe County)
Died: March 11, 1919 Aged: 64y Born: Virginia Buried: March 13, 1919
Father: Thomas Carr (VA) Mother: Ellen Burkett (VA) Status: Widowed
Carter, William Edward (Book 2B Page 320 Monroe County)
Died: March 19, 1919 Aged: 4m 1d Born: November 18, 1918 in Buxton, Iowa
Buried: March 20, 1919 Father: William Edward Carter (IL) Mother: Susie Carpenter
Casey, Geo. M. (Book 2B Page 337 Monroe County)
Died: June 14, 1919 Aged: 69y 13d Born: June 1, 1850 in Virginia
Buried: June 17, 1919 Father: Unnamed Mother: Unnamed Status: Widowed
Cattern, Wm. Jasper (Book 1 1897-1935 Monroe County)
Died: February 25, 1902 Aged: 6m 25d Born: Ottumwa, Iowa
Buried: Not Given Father: Unnamed Mother: Unnamed
Cheffee, Susan Lawson (1906- 1911 Mahaska County)
Died: September 30, 1910 Aged: Not Given Born: May 13, 1885 in Virginia
Buried: Not Given Father: Not Given Mother: Not Given

D:

Doyle, Eliza (Book 2A Page 57 Monroe County)
Died: March 6, 1907 Stillborn Born: March 6, 1907 in Iowa Buried: March 6, 1907
Father: Peter Doyle (VA) Mother: Bell Carr
Dickson, Fanny (Book 2A Page 82 Monroe County)
Died: July 11, 1907 Aged: 25y 3m 9d Born: April 2, 1882 in Missouri
Buried: July 12, 1907 Father: Unnamed Ramsey Mother: Sarah Ramsey
DeVorce, Unnamed (Book 2A Page 115 Monroe County)
Died: January 5, 1908 Stillborn Born: January 5, 1908 in Iowa Buried: January 5, 1908
Father: Lee DeVorce (AL) Mother: Mamie Johnson
Doyle, Louie (Book 2A Page 168 Monroe County)
Died: January 27, 1909 Aged: Not Given Born: November 24, 1908 in Iowa
Buried: January 28, 1909 Father: Peter Doyle (VA) Mother: Mary Bell
Davenport, Henry (Book 2A Page 246 Monroe County)
Died: March 25, 1911 Aged: abt 42y Born: Kentucky Buried: March 29, 1911
Father: Unnamed Mother: Unnamed Status: Widowed
Deering, Infant (Book 2A Page 258 Monroe County)
Died: May 23, 1911 Aged: 28d Born: April 23, 1911 in Iowa Buried: May 23, 1911
Father: Handy Deering (VA) Mother: Mammie Simmons
Davis, Millie (Book 2A Page 333 Monroe County)
Died: May 1, 1912 Aged: abt 39y Born: Virginia Buried: May 3, 1912
Father: Unknown Mother: Francis Tucker Status: Married

East First Street, from the intersection with Main Street. The first company store is at center left, the YMCA is at right. (Monroe County Historical Museum.)

Downs, Edward (Book 2A Page 437 Monroe County)
Died: January 25, 1914 Aged: 37y Born: Pennsylvania Buried: January 27, 1914
Father: Robert Downs (PA) Mother: Nancy

DeSleet, Nella G. (Book 2B Page 115 Monroe County)
Died: May 4, 1916 Aged: 19y 10m 14d Born: Ohio Buried: May 6, 1916
Father: Nelson DeSleet (OH) Mother: Sarah Jackson

Dyke, Baby (Book 2B Page 231 Monroe County)
Died: April 23, 1918 Aged: 12d Born: April 12, 1918 in Buxton, Iowa
Buried: April 23, 1918 Father: Aaron Dyke (Holland) Mother: Ruby May Pneuer

Dickson, Theodor (Book 2A Page 41 Monroe County)
Died: January 7, 1907 Aged: 10m 25d Born: March 13, 1906 in Alabama
Buried: January 9, 1907 Father: Geo. Dickson (AL) Mother: Sarah Kennedy

E:

Elligan, Unnamed (Book 2A Page 129 Monroe County)
Died: April 25, 1908 Aged: 10d Born: April 15, 1908 in Iowa Buried: April 26, 1908
Father: Jas. Elligan (MO) Mother: Emma Procter

Ewing, Infant (Book 2A Page 327 Monroe County)
Died: April 9, 1912 Stillborn Born: April 9, 1912 in Iowa Buried: April 10, 1912
Father: Robert Ewing (MO) Mother: Lucy Jones

Ellis, James T. (Book 2A Page 428 Monroe County)
Died: November 4, 1913 Aged: 73y 4m 25d Born: June 29, 1840 in Virginia
Buried: November 6, 1913 Father: Unnamed Mother: Mary

Ewing, Lucy Luiza (Book 2B Page 39 Monroe County)
Died: March 9, 1915 Aged: 49y 10m 26d Born: April 11, 1865 in Virginia
Buried: March 11, 1915 Father: Jackson Jones (VA) Mother: Sallie Martin

F:

Floyd, Ervin (Book 2A Page 97 Monroe County)
Died: October 4, 1907 Aged: 50y 7m 24d Born: March 10, 1857 in Georgia
Buried: October 6, 1907 Father: Unnamed Mother: Unnamed
Fergeson, Lewis (Book 2A Page 306 Monroe County)
Died: January 3, 1912 Aged: 73y 9d Born: December 25 in Virginia
Buried: January 5, 1912 Father: Unnamed Mother: Unnamed
Fargay, Fred (Book 2B Page 239 Monroe County)
Died: May 26, 1918 Aged: 43y 9m 28d Born: July 28, 1874 in West Virginia
Buried: May 30, 1918 Father: John Fargay (VA) Mother: Sallie Morris
Fields, Hermis (1906- 1911 Mahaska County)
Died: June 24, 1907 Aged: Not Given Born: July 30, 1904
Buried: Not Given Father: Not Given Mother: Not Given

G:

Graves, Jordon
Died: February 1, 1902 Aged: 39y Born: Pennsylvania Co., Virginia
Gaines, Reuben (Garland VanArkel Langkamp Funeral Home- Mahaska County)
Died: October 7, 1922 Aged: 62y 9m 26d Born: Virginia
Glass, Sylvanis (Book 2A Page 13 Monroe County)
Died: September 8, 1906 Aged: 4m 28d Born: April 11, 1896 in Iowa
Buried: September 9, 1906 Father: T.S. Glass (GA) Mother: Mary J. Glenn
Grevious, Jessie W. (Book 2A Page 42 Monroe County)
Died: January 22, 1907 Aged: 1y 5m Born: September 5, 1905 in Iowa
Buried: January 24, 1907 Father: H. Grevious (VA) Mother: Cornelius Brown
Grimes, Levi (Book 2A Page 49 Monroe County)
Died: February 22, 1907 Aged: 11y 11m 27d Born: February 23, 1895 in Iowa
Buried: February 24, 1907 Father: James Grimes (TN) Mother: Maggie Harris
Graves, Lee (Book 2A Page 64 Monroe County)
Died: April 25, 1907 Stillborn Born: April 25, 1907 Buried: April 26, 1907
Father: Lee Graves (VA) Mother: Helen Coles
Glass, Unnamed (Book 2A Page 87 Monroe County)
Died: August 3, 1907 Aged: 4m 27d Born: April 7, 1907 in Iowa Buried: August 4, 1907
Father: T.S. Glass (GA) Mother: Mamie J. Glenn
Green, Estella (Book 2A Page 124 Monroe County)
Died: March 20, 1908 Aged: 1y 9m Born: March 11, 1907 in Iowa
Buried: March 22, 1908 Father: Jack Green (AL) Mother: L. Rodgers
Guy, Mrs. Eva A. (Book 2A Page 220 Monroe County)
Died: October 10, 1910 Aged: 26y 11m 5d Born: November 5, 1883 in Iowa
Buried: October 13, 1910 Father: John Ampey (VA) Mother: Lulu Harris

Graves, Dorothy (Book 2A Page 299 Monroe County)
Died: December 19, 1911 Aged: 9m 5d Born: March 12, 1911 in Iowa
Buried: December 20, 1911 Father: Unknown Mother: Mary Graves
Graves, Elsie M. (Book 2A Page 368 Monroe County)
Died: January 25, 1913 Aged: 19y 9m 5d Born: April 20, 1894 in West Virginia
Buried: January 27, 1913 Father: Lee Graves (WVA) Mother: Hellen Coles
Garnett, Emery (Book 2A Page 381 Monroe County)
Died: March 9, 1913 Aged: 15d Born: February 22, 1913 in Buxton, Iowa
Buried: March 10, 1913 Father: Unknown Mother: Bertha Garnett
Graves, John H. (Book 2A Page 438 Monroe County)
Died: January 27, 1914 Aged: 52y Born: Virginia Buried: January 30, 1914
Father: George Graves (VA) Mother: Mildred Roares Status: Married
Green, Mrs. Ada (Book 2A Page 439 Monroe County)
Died: January 26, 1914 Aged: 39y Born: Missouri Buried: January 28, 1914
Father: Bevly Lay (MD) Mother: Emily Austin
Gowin, James (Book 2B Page 2 Monroe County)
Died: July 29, 1914 Aged: abt 55y Born: Not Given Buried: July 31, 1914
(No one knows him or anything about him)
Graves, John W. (Book 2B Page 2 Monroe County)
Died: July 29, 1914 Aged: 12y 1m 17d Born: June 12, 1902 in Iowa
Buried: August 1, 1914 Father: John Graves (VA) Mother: Bell Harrell
Graves, Jessie (Book 2B Page 6 Monroe County)
Died: August 10, 1914 Aged: 3y 3m 17d Born: April 24, 1911 in Iowa
Buried: August 10, 1914 Father: John W. Graves (VA) Mother: Bell Harrell
Graves, Josie (Book 2B Page 6 Monroe County)
Died: August 10, 1914 Aged: 15y 2m 2d Born: June 8, 1899 in Iowa
Buried: August 11, 1914 Father: John W. Graves (VA) Mother: Bell Harrell
Graves, Paul (Book 2B Page 6 Monroe County)
Died: August 9, 1914 Aged: 5y 9m 4d Born: November 5, 1909 in Iowa
Buried: August 9, 1914 Father; John W. Graves (VA) Mother: Bell Harrell
Graves, Thelma (Book 2B Page 6 Monroe County)
Died: August 5, 1914 Aged: 1y 8m 29d Born: November 7, 1912 in Iowa
Buried: August 6, 1914 Father: John W. Graves (VA) Mother: Bell Harrell
Gardon, Emma Lee (Book 2B Page 59 Monroe County)
Died: June 14, 1915 Aged: 19y 10m 4d Born: August 10, 1895 in Alabama
Buried: June 16, 1915 Father: Steve Crawford (AL) Mother: Hattie Head
Granison, Meridith (Book 2B Page 131 Monroe County)
Died: August 28, 1916 Aged: 62y 8m 14d Born: March 14, 1854
Buried: August 31, 1916 Father: Unknown Mother: Unknown Status: Married
Gibbons, William E. (Book 2B Page 192 Monroe County)
Died: September 27, 1917 Aged: 2m 6d Born: July 21, 1917 in Iowa Buried: September 28, 1917
Father: William Edward Gibbons (IA) Mother: Mettie Gordon
Garrett, Joe Jr. (Book 2B Page 220 Monroe County)
Died: February 23, 1918 Aged: 1y 7m 25d Born: June 28, 1916 in Buxton, Iowa
Buried: Febraury 26, 1918 Father: Joe Garrett (AK) Mother: Daisy Anderson

Garrett, Beatrice Bernice (Book 2B Page 225 Monroe County)
Died: March 9, 1918 Aged: 3y 7m 23d Born: July 14, 1914 in Iowa
Buried: March 10, 1918 Father: Joe Garrett (AK) Mother: Daisy Anderson
Garrett, Warren Andrew (Book 2B Page 225 Monroe County)
Died: March 21, 1918 Aged: 1m 19d Born: February 2, 1918 in Consol, Iowa
Buried: March 23, 1918 Father: Joe Garrett (AK) Mother: Daisy Anderson
Gaines, Moses (Book 2B Page 240 Monroe County)
Died: May 12, 1918 Aged: 62y 8m 15d Born: August 28, 1855 in Virginia
Buried: May 14, 1918 Father: Unknown Mother: Unknown Informant: Lenard Gaines
Griggs, John (Book 2B Page 332 Monroe County)
Died; May 23, 1919 Aged: 64y 2m 19d Born: March 4, 1855 in Michigan
Buried: May 24, 1919 Father: Unknown Mother: Unknown

H:

Harper, Wm. Henry
Died: August 16, 1903 Aged: 1y 2m Born: Bluff Creek Twp. Monroe County
Buried: Not Given Father: Unnamed Mother: Unnamed
Harris, Simon
Died: November 5, 1903 Aged: 54y 6m Born: Fluvania Co., Virginia
Buried: Not Given Father: Unnamed Mother: Unnamed
Hackett, Minnie (Book 2A Page 7 Monroe County)
Died: August 6, 1906 Aged: 13y 4d Born: August 2, 1893 in Maryland
Buried: August 8, 1906 Father: Geo. Hackett (MD) Mother: Mary Henry
Hale, Polly (Book 2A Page 21 Monroe County)
Died: October 19, 1906 Aged: 40y Born: June 1866 in Virginia
Buried: October 22, 1906 Father: Jerry Wilson (VA) Mother: Bettie Gains
Harvey, Francis (Book 2A Page 21 Monroe County)
Died: October 6, 1906 Aged: 9m Born: January 12, 1906 Buried: October 7, 1906
Father: Irvie Harvey Mother: Eliz McCane
Hartwell, Jack (Book 2A Page 42 Monroe County)
Died: January 11, 1907 Aged: 32y 3m 6d Born: October 5, 1875 in Virginia
Buried: January 15, 1907 Father: Jace Hartwell (VA) Mother: Julia Unnamed
Hanley, Joseph (Book 2A Page 58 Monroe County)
Died: March 31, 1907 Aged: 6y 9m 18d Born: August 12, 1901 in Maryland
Buried: April 1, 1907 Father: Joseph Hanley (NC) Mother: Rachel Pendleton
Hawkins, Laura L. (Book 2A Page 92 Monroe County)
Died: September 28, 1907 Aged: 57y 10m 13d Born: November 15, 1850 in Virginia
Buried: October 1, 1907 Father: Ben Watson (VA) Mother: Sofa Watson
Hanley, Unnamed (Book 2A Page 101 Monroe County)
Died: November 28, 1907 Aged: 3y 10d Born: November 18, 1904 in Maryland
Buried: November 30, 1907 Father: Joseph Hanley (NC) Mother: Rachel Pendleton
Hurst, T. (Book 2A Page 112 Monroe County)
Died: January 6, 1908 Aged: 1y 1d Born: January 5, 1907 in Iowa
Buried: January 8, 1908 Father: A.C. Hurst (OH) Mother: Lulu Hammond

Hill, Wallace (Book 2A Page 162 Monroe County)
Died: December 22, 1908 Aged: 46y 9m Born: March 1862 in Virginia
Buried: December 24, 1908 Father: Tom Hill (VA) Mother: Unnamed
Heartwell, Jack (Book 2A Page 205 Monroe County)
Died: July 28, 1910 Aged: abt 68y Born: Virginia Buried: July 30, 1910
Father: Unnamed Mother: Unnamed
Hurst, Zelma M. (Book 2A Page 227 Monroe County)
Died: November 18, 1910 Aged: 2y 1m Born: October 5, 1908 in Iowa
Buried: November 20, 1910 Father: A.C. Hurst (OH) Mother: Lottie Hurst
Hill, Zenobia (Book 2A Page 241 Monroe County)
Died: February 2, 1911 Aged: 5m 8d Born: September 10, 1910 in Iowa
Buried: February 4, 1911 Father: C.L. Hill (IA) Mother: Unnamed Gains
Harris, Susan B. (Book 2A Page 270 Monroe County)
Died: July 13, 1911 Aged: abt 80y Born: Virginia Buried: July 18, 1911
Father: Unnamed Mother: Unnamed
Hawkins, Thos. Vincon (book 2A Page 277 Monroe County)
Died: August 16, 1911 Aged: 1y 8m 8d Born; December 7, 1909 in Iowa
Buried: August 18, 1911 Father: Henry Hawkins (VA) Mother: Unnamed Vincon
Hart, Hellena (Book 2A Page 327 Monroe County)
Died: April 28, 1912 Aged: 1y 3m 4d Born: January 24, 1911 in Iowa
Buried: April 30, 1912 Father: Robert Hart (VA) Mother: Ella Blackburn
Harris, Lucy (Book 2A Page 334 Monroe County)
Died: May 3, 1912 Aged: 28y Born: Virginia Buried: May 5, 1912
Father: Louis Thornton (VA) Mother: Sallie Thornton
Hurst, Syrus (Book 2A Page 352 Monroe County)
Died: September 15, 1912 Aged: 17y 3d Born: September 27, 1895
Buried: September 17, 1912 Father: A.C. Hurst (OH) Mother: Lula Hammond
Hogsette, Olaf (Book 2A Page 469 Monroe County)
Died: June 22, 1914 Aged: 20y 9m 22d Born: August 31, 1894 in Iowa
Buried: June 25, 1914 Father: Sherman Hogsette (VA) Mother: Eliza Johnson
Henderson, Oscar M. (Book 2B Page 111 Monroe County)
Died: April 8, 1916 Aged: abt 50y Born: abt 1866 in Virginia
Buried: April 10, 1916 Father: Unknown Mother: Unknown
Henderson, J.H. (Book 2B Page 147 Monroe County)
Died: November 6, 1916 Aged: abt 66y Born: Unknown
Buried: November 9, 1916 Father: Unknown Mother: Unknown
Harper, William (Book 2B Page 315 Monroe County)
Died: February 1, 1919 Aged: abt 50y Born: Unknown in Tennessee
Buried: February 3, 1919 Father: Unknown Mother: Unknown

I:

Irvin, Chas. (Book 2A Page 452 Monroe County)
Died: March 20, 1914 Aged: 50y Born: Virginia Buried: March 23, 1914
Father: Stephen Irvin (VA) Mother: Emma Irvin

J:

Jewett, Alfred
Died: April 28, 1902 Aged: 64y 4m Born: Albamarle Co., Virginia
Buried: Not Listed Father: Unknown Mother: Unknown
Johnson, Lola M.
Died: December 14, 1908 Aged: 2y 8m 15d Born: March 29, 1906 in Iowa
Buried; December 19, 1908 Father: Richard Johnson (MO) Mother: Fanny MicKim
Johnson, Infant (Book 2A Page 3 Monroe County)
Died: July 1, 1906 Aged: 21d Born: June 11, 1906 in Iowa Buried: July 2, 1906
Father: Wm. Johnson Mother: Unnamed
Johnson, Ned (1906- 1911 Mahaska County)
Died: January 23, 1910 Aged: abt 54y Born: Virginia
Buried: Not Given Father: Not Given Mother: Not Given
Jackson, Martin (Book 2A Page 22 Monroe County)
Died: October 15, 1906 Aged: 56y Born: November 2, 1850 in Missouri
Buried: October 15, 1906 Father: Unnamed Jackson Mother: Caroline
Jones, Ann (Book 2A Page 22 Monroe County)
Died: October 15, 1906 Aged: 70y 9m 20d Born; December 24, 1835 in Wales
Buried: October 17, 1906 Father: James Jones (Wales) Mother: Eliz. Jones
Jones, Walter (Book 2A Page 43 Monroe County)
Died: January 10, 1907 Aged: 7m Born: April 15, 1906 in Iowa
Buried: January 12, 1907 Father: Ben Jones (VA) Mother: Lillie Pollard
Jackson, Early F. (Book 2A Page 59 Monore County)
Died: March 13, 1907 Aged: 22y 1m 7d Born: February 22, 1885 in Missouri
Buried: March 17, 1907 Father: Wm. Taylor (MO) Mother: Ellen Allen
Johnson, Anna M. (Book 2A Page 76 Monroe County)
Died: June 24, 1907 Aged: 4m Born: February 2, 1907 in Iowa
Buried: June 25, 1907 Father: A.J. Johnson (IA) Mother: Ella Tolliver
Johnson, Henry (Book 2A Page 107 Monroe County)
Died: December 20, 1907 Aged: 21y 11m Born: February 20, 1886 in Indiana
Buried: December 22, 1907 Father: Dick Johnson (KY) Mother: Victoria Carter
Jobes, Elverta (Book 2A Page 112 Monroe County)
Died: January 15, 1908 Aged: 21y 9m Born: May
Buried: January 18, 1908 Father: Z.R. Williams (VA) Mother: Laura Riggs
Jackson, Andrew (Book 2A Page 118 Monroe County)
Died: February 13, 1908 Aged: 63y Born: Virginia Buried: February 16, 1908
Father: Martin R. Jackson (LA) Mother; Caroline Jackson
Johnson, Ollie M. (Book 2A Page 125 Monroe County)
Died: March 7, 1908 Aged: 2y 17d Born: February 21, 1906 in Missouri
Buried: March 9, 1908 Father: B. Johnson (VA) Mother: T. Brown
Jackson, Mary Jane (Book 2A Page 174 Monroe County)
Died: February 15, 1909 Aged: 62y 1m 14d Born: January 1, 1847 in Virginia
Buried: February 18, 1909 Father: Joe Williams (VA) Mother: Charity Williams
Johnson, John (Book 2A Page 194 Monroe County)
Died: May 26, 1909 Aged: 43y 28d Born: April 28, 1866 in Kentucky
Buried: May 29, 1909 Father: Alfred Johnson (KY) Mother: Margaret Ritta

Jones, Hattie (Book 2A Page 200 Monroe County)
Died: June 25, 1909 Aged: 20y 11m 21d Born: July 4, 1889 in Tennessee
Buried: June 27, 1909 Father: Robert Powell Mother: Mary Coleman
Johnson, Willard J. (Book 2A Page 210 Monroe County)
Died: August 2, 1910 Aged: 2m 16d Born: May 16, 1910 in Iowa
Buried: August 3, 1910 Father: R.J. Johnson (WVA) Mother: Ella Wallace
Jones, Shimetta (Book 2A Page 215 Monroe County)
Died: September 30, 1910 Aged: 5m Born: May 2, 1910 in Iowa
Buried: October 2, 1910 Father: Henry Jones (VA) Mother: Cleo. Dorsey
Johnson, Albert (Book 2A Page 254 Monroe County)
Died: April 21, 1911 Aged: 24y 11m 13d Born: June 5 in Iowa
Buried: April 23, 1911 Father: Robert Johnson (IA) Mother: Hannah Johnson
James, Rossie B. (Book 2A Page 307 Monroe County)
Died: January 29, 1912 Aged: 15 hours Born: January 29, 1912 in Iowa
Buried: January 30, 1912 Father: Bernie A. James (WVA) Mother: Evelyn Willis
Jewett, Ioola (Book 2A Page 328 Monroe County)
Died: April 20, 1912 Aged: 7m 20d Born: August 27, 1911 in Iowa
Buried: April 22, 1912 Father: Wm. Jewett (IA) Mother: Margaret Ampey
Jones, Howard Richard (Book 2A Page 328 Monroe County)
Died: April 20, 1912 Aged: 2d Born: April 18, 1912 Buried: April 23, 1912
Father: Adolph Jones (IA) Mother: Alice Brown
Jones, Mrs. Lilly (Book 2A Page 398 Monroe County)
Died: June 3, 1913 Aged: 30y 7m 21d Born: November 24, 1883 in Virginia
Buried: June 5, 1913 Father: Buffan Pollard (VA) Mother: Mandy Pollard
Jones, Rudolph (Book 2A Page 408 Monroe County)
Died: August 27, 1913 Aged: 1m 23d Born: July 4, 1913 in Iowa
Buried: August 28, 1913 Father: C.P. Jones (IA) Mother: Lulu Ellis
Jackson, Janie (Book 2A Page 413 Monroe County)
Died: September 25, 1913 Aged: 1y 1m 5d Born: August 12, 1912
Buried: September 28, 1913 Father: Henry M. Jackson (OH) Mother: Lizzy Weston
Jones, Floyd (Book 2B Page 136 Monroe County)
Died: September 2, 1916 Aged: 52y 2m 25d Born: June 8, 1884 in North Carolina
Buried: September 4, 1916 Father: Lloyd Jones Mother: Unnamed
James, Wilson J.B. (Book 2B Page 163 Monroe County) - Murdered
Died: February 13, 1917 Aged: 25y 4m 15d Born: September 28, 1891 in Iowa
Buried: February 16, 1917 Father: Wilson James (VA) Mother: Sallie Exrozier
James, Wilson (Book 2B Page 183 Monroe County)
Died: July 10, 1917 Aged: 66y 7m 9d Born: December 1, 1850 in Virginia
Buried: July 13, 1917 Father: Peater James (VA) Mother: Unnamed
Jackson, Herbert (Book 2B Page 226 Monroe County)
Died: March 13, 1918 Aged: 17y 2m 21d Born: December 20, 1900 in Iowa
Buried: March 15, 1918 Father: Unnamed Mother: Unnamed Informant: Laura White
Jenkins, Flora I/L. (Book 2B Page 233 Monroe County)
Died: April 7, 1918 Aged: 19y 9m 28d Born: June 10, 1899 in Pana, Illinois
Buried: April 9, 1918 Father: John Wilson (Canada) Mother: Mary Oliphant

Jenkins, Mildred Hester (Book 2B Page 271 Monroe County)
Died: October 7, 1918 Aged: 6m 8d Born: March 29, 1918 in Buxton, Iowa
Buried: October 9, 1918 Father: Samuel James Jenkins (MO) Mother: Flora L. Wilson
Jones, Franklin Taylor
Died: November 23, 1922 Aged: 3m 24d Born: Not Given Buried: November 29, 1922
Father: E.F. Jones (IA) Mother: Gladys Smith (KY)
Johnson, James (1911- 1915 Mahaska County)
Died: April 22, 1915 Aged: Not Given Born: December 14, 1885 in Iowa
Buried: Not Given Father: Not Given Mother: Not Given

K:

Kenedy, Mary Ida
Died: October 16, 1903 Aged: 23y Born: Hillsville, Virginia Buried: Not Given
Father: Not Given Mother: Not Given (Killed by J.C. Smith)
King, Ethel (Book 2A Page 289 Monroe County)
Died: October 8, 1911 Aged: abt 21y Born: Iowa Buried: October 10, 1911
Father: John King (VA) Mother: Mary King

L:

Lippard, Richard
Died: April 11, 1902 Aged: 2y 11m Born: Montgomery Co., Virginia
Buried: Not Given Father: Unnamed Mother: Unnamed
Louis, Lee Drew (Book 2A Page Monroe County)
Died: August 10, 1906 Aged: 7m 5d Born: January 6, 1906 in Iowa
Buried: August 11, 1906 Father: Walter Louis (VA) Mother: Sallie Mitchell
Lynch, Richard (Book 2A Page 30 Monroe County)
Died: November 15, 1906 Aged: 3m 15d Born: July 30, 1906 in Iowa
Buried: November 15, 1906 Father: J.F. Lynch (AL) Mother: Nora Garren
Lewis, Lex H. (Book 2A Page 43 Monroe County)
Died: January 16, 1907 Aged: 1 week Born: January 9, 1907 in Iowa
Buried: January 17, 1907 Father: Walter Lewis (VA) Mother: Sally Harris
Lynch, Unnamed (Book 2A Page 88 Monroe County)
Died: August 5, 1907 Stillborn Born: August 5, 1907 Buried: August 5, 1907
Father: J.F. Lynch (AL) Mother: Nora Garvin
Lee, Sadia G. (Book 2A Page 113 Monroe County)
Died: January 15, 1908 Aged: 8m 8d Born: April 28, 1907 in Iowa
Buried: January 17, 1908 Father: W.W. Lee (VA) Mother: Alberta Pugh
Lee, Helen (Book 2A Page 188 Monroe County)
Died: April 2, 1909 Aged: 4m 6d Born: December 16, 1908 Buried: April 23, 1909
Father: Wm. Lee (VA) Mother: Alberta Malvina Pugh
Lee, John W. (Book 2A Page 231 Monroe County)
Died: December 24, 1910 Aged: 3d Born: December 21, 1910 in Iowa
Buried: December 24, 1910 Father: George Lee (NC) Mother: Esther Jones

Above and right: Panorama of Buxton Cemetery while cleaning was underway in 2002.

Lee, W.W. (Book 2A Page 422 Monroe County)
Died: October 16, 1913 Aged: 42y 10m 9d Born: December 7 in Virginia
Buried: October 19, 1913 Father: Martin Lee (VA) Mother: Hattie Strother
Lawson, Lina (Book 2A Page 434 Monroe County)
Died: December 26, 1913 Aged: 33y 3m Born: 1880 in Virginia
Buried: December 28, 1913 Father: Sam West (VA) Mother: Virginia Unnamed
Lyons, C.J. (Book 2A Page 453 Monroe County)
Died: March 19, 1914 Aged: abt 45y Born: Tennessee Buried: March 22, 1914
Father: Unknown Mother: Unknown
Lee, Melvina Alberta (Book 2B Page 22 Monroe County)
Died: December 28, 1914 Aged: 31y 19d Born: December 9, 1883 in Iowa
Buried: December 29, 1914 Father: Chas. Pugh (MO) Mother: Susie Jones
Logan, Mazura (Book 2B Page 50 Monroe County)
Died: May 8, 1915 Aged: 48y 2d Born: May 6, 1867 in Virginia
Buried: May 1915 Father: Thos. Hodds (VA) Mother: Betty Howser

M:

Miller, Sallie
Died: August 15, 1923 Aged: abt 58y Born: Not Given Buried: August 17, 1923
Father: Not Given Mother: Not Given Status: Married
McKinney, James
Died: September 19, 1923 Aged: abt 50y Born: Not Given Buried: September 21, 1923
Father: Not Given Mother: Not Given Status: Widowed

LeeAnn Dickey

(Dickey collection.)

Mauson, Mary
Died: August 31, 1902 Aged: 58y 3m 24d Born: Albemarle Co., Virginia
Father: Not Given Mother: Not Given Status: Not Given

Miller, Mrs. Margaret
Died: January 11, 1911 Aged: 29y 3m 11d Born: October 20, 1881 in Alabama
Buried: January 15, 1911 Father: Harry Head (AL) Mother: Lizzy Head

Massey, Horace (Book 2A Page 4 Monroe County)
Died: July 19, 1906 Aged: 41y 11m 14d Born: August 5, 1861 in Virginia
Buried: July 22, 1906 Father: Henry Massey (VA) Mother: Polly Rhodes

Miller, Unnamed (Book 2A Page 31 Monroe County)
Died: November 8, 1906 Stillborn Born: November 8, 1906 Buried: November 9, 1906
Father: G.A. Miller (KY) Mother: Pearl Ward

Mason, John W. (Book 2A Page 65 Monroe County)
Died: April 10, 1907 Aged: 40y Born: Virginia Buried: April 12, 1907
Father: Unnamed Mother: Catherine Hearth

McDanel, Eva (Book 2A Page 65 Monroe County)
Died: April 13, 1907 Aged: 1y 8m 10d Born: July 3, 1906 in Iowa
Buried: J.M. McDanel (TN) Mother: Fanny Murphy

Milton, Unnamed (Book 2A Page 93 Monroe County)
Died: September 3, 1907 Aged: 1m 1d Born: August 12, 1907 in Iowa
Buried: September 14, 1907 Father: Frank Milton (AL) Mother: Silla Larkin

Mason, Beatrice (Book 2A Page 108 Monroe County)
Died: December 25, 1907 Aged: 5m 24d Born: August 1, 1907 in Iowa
Buried: December 26, 1907 Father: J.W. Mason (VA) Mother: Lulu Frazier

Murray, Vernon (Book 2A Page 147 Monroe County)
Died: September 23, 1908 Aged: 11m 4d Born: October 19, 1907 in Iowa
Buried: September 25, 1908 Father: A. Murray (VA) Mother: Rachel Power

Moppin, Grace (Book 2A Page 152 Monroe County)
Died: October 28, 1908 Aged: 53y 6m 4d Born: April 24, 1855 in Virginia
Buried: November 1, 1908 Father: Winston Carter (VA) Mother: Martha Carter
Moman, James (Book 2A Page 201 Monroe County)
Died: June 19, 1909 Aged: 43y Born: Not Given Buried: June 20, 1909
Father: James Moman Mother: Not Given
McDonald, Robert (Book 2A Page 215 Monroe County)
Died: September 5, 1910 Aged: 1y 7m Born: February 1, 1909 in Alabama
Buried: September 6, 1910 Father: Robert McDonald (AL) Mother: Josie Harrison
Massey, Annie J. (Book 2A Page 216 Monroe County)
Died: September 29, 1910 Aged: 5m 28d Born: April 2, 1919 in Iowa
Buried: September 30, 1910 Father: Nick Massey (VA) Mother: Gertrude Jones
Mease, Leo Hobart (Book 2A Page 242 Monroe County)
Died: February 23, 1911 Aged: 16y 10d Born: February 13, 1896 in Iowa
Buried: February 25, 1911 Father: Charlie H. Mease (VA) Mother: Cornelia Fannie Tate
Morrison, Melva (Book 2A Page 335 Monroe County)
Died: May 18, 1912 Aged: 1y 1m 16d Born: March 2, 1911 in Iowa
Buried: May 20, 1912 Father: William C. Morrison (MO) Mother: Georgia Wright
Mickens, Mrs. Mary (Book 2A Page 347 Monroe County)
Died: August 15, 1912 Aged: abt 60y Born: Virginia Buried: August 18, 1912
Father: Not Given Mother: Not Given
Miller, Brisco (Book 2A Page 364 Monroe County)
Died: December 20, 1912 Aged: abt 61y Born: Not Given Buried: December 23, 1912
Father: Not Given Mother: Not Given
Morgan, Infant (Book 2A Page 365 Monroe County)
Died: December 29, 1912 Stillborn Born: December 29, 1912
Buried: December 30, 1912 Father: Wm. Morgan (VA) Mother: Ella Peg/ Pig
McKinnie, Mrs. Effie (Book 2A Page 390 Monroe County)
Died: April 7, 1913 Aged: 29y 11m 28d Born: May 5, 1884 in Virginia
Buried: April 9, 1913 Father: Jacob Brown (VA) Mother: Jennie Frazier Status: Divorced
Morgan, James P. (Book 2A Page 399 Monroe County)
Died: June 18, 1913 Aged: 2y 11m 20d Born: July 8, 1911 in Iowa
Buried: June 19, 1913 Father: Wm. Morgan (VA) Mother: Ella Peg/ Pig
Michael, Cortelia (Book 2A Page 423 Monroe County)
Died: October 19, 1913 Aged: 40y 3m 20d Born: June 30, 1873 in North Carolina
Buried: October 22, 1913 Father: John Weston (NC) Mother: Mattie Hamilton
Mathews, Stewart (Book 2A Page 453 Monroe County)
Died: March 22, 1914 Aged: 60y Born: March 10, 1854 in Virginia
Buried: March 25, 1914 Father: Unknown Mother: Unknown
Miller, Fanny May (Book 2A Page 471 Monroe County)
Died: June 16, 1914 Aged: 14y 3m 12d Born: March 4, 1900 in Illinois
Buried: June 18, 1914 Father: Harry W. Miller (TN) Mother: Lucy Pane
Morgan, Infant (Book 2B Page 14 Monroe County)
Died: October 12, 1914 Aged: 4 hours Born: October 12, 1914 in Buxton, Iowa
Buried: October 14, 1914 Father: Wm. Morgan (VA) Mother: Ella Pigg

Marshall, Hill (Book 2B Page 41 Monroe County)
Died: March 6, 1915 Aged: 60y 6m 20d Born: August 15, 1854 in Georgia
Buried: March 7, 1915 Father: Unknown Mother: Unknown Status: Divorced
McKemson, Maxine (Book 2B Page 170 Monroe County)
Died: March 22, 1917 Stillborn Born: March 22, 1917 Buried: March 22, 1917
Father: Unknown Mother: Myrtle Unknown Informant: Westelly Garnett
Miller, George W. (Book 2B page 194 Monroe County)
Died: September 10, 1917 Aged: 76y 8d Born: September 2, 1841 in North Carolina
Buried: September 12, 1917 Father: Peate Miller Mother: Unnamed
McKinney, Bernice (Book 2B Page 249 Monroe County)
Died: June 24, 1918 Aged: 6y 10m 17d Born: August 7, 1911 in Greenridge, Iowa
Buried: June 26, 1918 Father: Norman McKinney (AL) Mother: Effie Brown
Mascara, Antonie (Book 2B Page 284 Monroe County)
Died: November 11, 1918 Aged: 24y 1m 15d Born: October 2, 1894 in Italy
Buried: November 20, 1918 Father: Phillipa Mascara (Italy) Mother: Teresa Carino
Minor, George Thomas (Book 2A Page 255 Monroe County)
Died: April 25, 1911 Aged: 57y Born: Vorginia Buried: April 30, 1911
Father: Unnamed Mother: Unnamed
Miachal, Ed Lee (1906- 1911 Mahaska County)
Died: November 16, 1910 Aged: Not Given Born: May 20, 1910 in Iowa
Buried: Not Given Father: Not Given Mother: Not Given
Mathew, William (1906- 1911 Mahaska County)
Died: July 15, 1910 Aged: Not Given Born: 1869 in Georgia
Buried: Not Given Father: Not Given Mother: Not Given
Michael, Mary E. (1906- 1911 Mahaska County)
Died: September 22, 1907 Aged: 70y Born: North Carolina
Buried: Not Given Father: Not Given Mother: Not Given
Muray, Tommy (1906- 1911 Mahaska County)
Died: December 7, 1908 Aged: Not Given Born: February 10, 1908 in Iowa
Buried: Not Given Father: Not Given Mother: Not Given
Michael, Frank (1911- 1915 Mahaska County)
Died: October 23, 1912 Aged: Not Given Born: June 26, 1912 in Iowa
Buried: Not Given Father: Not Given Mother: Not Given

N:

Novak, Mary (Book 2A Page 283 Monroe County)
Died: September 14, 1911 Aged: 11d Born: September 3, 1911 in Iowa
Buried: September 15, 1911 Father: John Novak (Bohemia) Mother: Pauline Rozum
Nichols, Rossie (Book 2A Page 330 Monroe County)
Died: April 3, 1912 Aged: 11y 0m 17d Born: March 16, 1901 in Iowa
Buried: April 5, 1912 Father: Robert Nichols (VA) Mother: Jane Gains
Norse, Jacob (Book 2B Page 84 Monroe County)
Died: December 14, 1915 Aged: 37y Born: 1878 in Alabama
Buried: December 16, 1915 Father: Samuel Norse (AL) Mother: Fannie Jones

O:

Oksji, Mary (Book 2A Page 354 Monroe County)
Died: September 29, 1912 Stillborn Born: September 29, 1912 in Buxton, Iowa Buried: September 30, 1912
Father: John Oskji (Austria) Mother: Mary Oskji
Oksji, Infant (Book 2A Page 416 Monroe County)
Died: September 25, 1913 Stillborn Born: September 25, 1913 in Iowa
Buried: September 25, 1913 Father: John Oskji (Austria) Mother: Anna Oskji
Oliphant, Caroline (Book 2A Page 455 Monroe County)
Died: March 4, 1914 Aged: 61y Born: Mississippi Buried: March 6, 1914
Father: Toby Oliphant Mother: Unknown
Onsley, Willie Belle (Book 2B Page 302 Monroe County)
Died: December 7, 1918 Aged: 5m 29d Born: June 8, 1918 in Buxton, Iowa
Buried: December 9, 1918 Father: Hugh Belle Onsley (IA) Mother: Lillian Lee (AL)
Onsley, Lillian (Book 2B Page 250 Monroe County)
Died: June 22, 1918 Aged: 24y 11m 28d Born: June 25, 1893 in Alabama
Buried: June 24, 1918 Father: Paul Crenbell (AL) Mother: Roxie Pompy (AL)

P:

Parker, Hattie (Book 2A Page 126 Monroe County)
Died: March 11, 1908 Aged: 25y 5m 15d Born: September 26, 1883 in Ohio
Buried: March 12, 1908 Father: Will Parker Mother: Maggie Johnson
Parker, Hattie (Book 2A Page 127 Monroe County)
Died: March 7, 1908 Aged: 6d Born: March 1, 1908 in Iowa
Buried: March 9, 1908 Father: Unnamed Mother: Hattie Parker
Parker, Dorothy (Book 2A Page 232 Monroe County)
Died: December 16, 1910 Aged: 2y 3m Born: September 28, 1908 in Iowa
Buried: December 17, 1910 Father: Harry Parker (OH) Mother: Cornelia Jackson
Parker, Henry Chas. (Book 2A Page 249 Monroe County)
Died: March 5, 1911 Aged: 4m 27d Born: October 9, 1910 in Iowa
Buried: March 6, 1911 Father: Harry Parker (OH) Mother: Cornelia Jackson
Pondexter, Rease (Book 2A Page 256 Monroe County)
Died: April 28, 1911 Aged: 79y Born: Virginia Buried: April 30, 1911
Father: Unnamed Mother: Unnamed
Patterson, William G. (Book 2A Page 360 Monroe County)
Died: November 10, 1912 Aged: 18y 4m 15d Born: June 25, 1894 in North Carolina
Buried: November 12, 1912 Father: George Patterson (NC) Mother: Mary Wallington
Parkey, Infant (Book 2A Page 448 Monroe County)
Died: February 20, 1914 Aged: 4d Born: February 17, 1914 in Iowa
Buried: February 21, 1914 Father: T.J. Parkey (TN) Mother: Emma Fish
Parkey, Walter (Book 2A Page 72 Monroe County)
Died: May 28, 1907 Aged: Not Given Born: August 22 in Kentucky
Buried: May 29, 1907 Father: T.J. Parkey (TN) Mother: Emma Fish

Poe, Add. (Book 2A Page 465 Monroe County)
Died: May 3, 1914 Aged: 35y 2m 2d Born: February 20, 1879 in Kentucky
Buried: May 5, 1914 Father: Green Poe (KY) Mother: Mary Keywood
Pugh, Infant (Book 2A Page 465 Monroe County)
Died: May 21, 1914 Stillborn Born: September 21, 1914 in Iowa
Buried: May 22, 1914 Father: Carl Pugh (KS) Mother: Eva Morrison
Price, Annie Bell (Book 2B Page 4 Monroe County)
Died: July 30, 1914 Aged: 52y 1m 21d Born: June 19, 1862 in Virginia
Buried: August 1, 1914 Father: John P. DeHaven (VA) Mother: Elizabeth DeHaven
Peaso, Samuel H. (Book 2B Page 59 Monroe County)
Died: July 12, 1915 Aged: 45y 7m 2d Born: December 10, 1869 in Virginia
Buried: July 15, 1915 Father: Thos. Peaso Mother: Unknown
Parker, Willy (Book 2B Page 73 Monroe County)
Died: October 10, 1915 Aged: 56y 10m 25d Born: November 15, 1858 in Virginia
Buried: October 13, 1915 Father: Unknown Mother: Unknown
Patterson, George (Book 2B Page 118 Monroe County)
Died: May 8, 1916 Aged: abt 63y Born: abt 1853 in North Carolina
Buried: May 10, 1916 Father: William Patterson (NC) Mother: Fannie Unnamed
Pollock, Geo. Dewey (Book 2B Page 118 Monroe County)
Died: May 14, 1916 Aged: 17y 5m 9d Born: December 5, 1898 in Iowa
Buried: May 16, 1916 Father: H.G. Pollock (OH) Mother: Mary E. Reeser
Pugh, Marry Frances (Book 2B Page 172 Monroe County)
Died: March 18, 1917 Stillborn Born: March 18, 1917 in Iowa
Buried: March 19, 1917 Father: J.B. Pugh (IA) Mother: Marry M. Byeyer
Prentice, Mrs. Samuel (1906- 1911 Mahaska County)
Died: October 14, 1907 Aged: Not Given Born: August 1858 in Iowa
Buried: Not Given Father: Not Given Mother: Not Given
Peterson, Herbert (1911- 1915 Mahaska County)
Died: February 3, 1913 Aged: Not Given Born: August 21, 1888 in Iowa
Buried: Not Given Father: Not Given Mother: Not Given

Q:

Qualls, Lefern (Book 2A Page 301 Monroe County)
Died: December 6, 1911 Aged: 1m Born: November 6, 1911 in Iowa
Buried: December 7, 1911 Father: Robert Qualls (IA) Mother: Jestina Carter

R:

Rhodes, Hubert Lincoln
Died: May 26, 1903 Aged: 6y Born: Munchakinock, Iowa
Buried: Not Given Father: Not Given Mother: Not Given
Robinson, Wm. A. (Book 2A Page 9 Monroe County)
Died: August 25, 1906 Aged: 7d Born: August 18, 1906 in Iowa
Buried: August 26, 1906 Father: W.A. Robinson (MO) Mother: Ella Williams

Robinson, Martha (Book 2A Page 37 Monroe County)
Died: December 6, 1906 Aged: 12y 9m Born: April 1894 in Iowa
Buried: December 9, 1906 Father: Ned Robinson (VA) Mother: Lue Price
Rhodes, Ernest (Book 2A Page 52 Monroe County)
Died: February 16, 1907 Aged: 11y Born: March 4, 1896 in Iowa
Buried: February 17, 1907 Father: Sam Rhodes (VA) Mother: Louisa Chattman
Robinson, Unnamed (Book 2A Page 66 Monroe County)
Died: April 16, 1907 Stillborn Born: April 16, 1907 Buried: April 17, 1907
Father: Ed Robinson (IA) Mother: Henrietta Webb
Reaves, Wm. H. (Book 2A Page 72 Monroe County)
Died: May 6, 1907 Aged: 63y Born: Not Given Buried: May 8, 1907
Father: Not Given Mother: Not Given
Reed, Leona (Book 2A Page 73 Monroe County)
Died: May 13, 1907 Aged: 25y 10m 9d Born: July 4, 1882 in North Carolina
Buried: May 13, 1907 Father: Unnamed Palmer Mother: Unnamed
Roberts, Jim (Book 2A Page 103 Monroe County)
Died: November 5, 1907 Aged: 54y 4m 1d Born: July 4, 1853 in Georgia
Buried: November 7, 1907 Father: Unnamed Mother: Lucinda Roberts
Roberts, Clem (Book 2A Page 114 Monroe County)
Died: January 18, 1908 Aged: 37y Born: Virginia Buried: January 19, 1908
Father: Not Given Mother: Not Given
Reaves, Elex (Book 2A Page 212 Monroe County)
Died: August 6, 1910 Aged: 55y Born: Virginia Buried: August 10, 1910
Father: Not Given Mother: Not Given
Richey, Clifford Odell (Book 2A Page 244 Monroe County)
Died: February 22, 1911 Aged: 3m 9d Born: November 13, 1910 in Iowa
Buried: February 23, 1911 Father: Andrew Richey (IA) Mother: Estella Jones
Randolph, John Wm. (Book 2A Page 256 Monroe County)
Died: April 14, 1911 Aged: 17y 1d Born: Illinois Buried: April 16, 1911
Father: John Randolph (VA) Mother: Mary Nadin
Rhoads, James Bill (Book 2A Page 261 Monroe County)
Died: May 1, 1911 Aged: 19y 10m 16d Born: June 5, 1891 in Iowa
Buried: May 4, 1911 Father: Samuel Rhoads (VA) Mother: Louisa Chattman
Ray, Florence (Book 2A Page 344 Monroe County)
Died: July 30, 1912 Aged: 6y 5m 4d Born: February 24, 1906 in Illinois
Buried: August 1, 1912 Father: Cairo Ray (KY) Mother: Eliza Frazier
Rhodes, Issac Leroy (Book 2A Page 355 Monroe County)
Died: September 4, 1912 Aged: 7m 4d Born: January 30, 1912 in Iowa
Buried: September 5, 1912 Father: W.B. Rhodes (VA) Mother: Mary Ragsdale
Rowlette, Mrs. G. (Gertrude) (Book 2A Page 384 Monroe County)
Died: March 13, 1913 Aged: 33y 1m 12d Born: February 2, 1880 in Arkansas
Buried: March 16, 1913 Father: Unknown Mother: Violet Scott
Rollette, Selestine M. (Book 2A Page 396 Monroe County)
Died: May 30, 1913 Aged: 10m 6d Born: July 25, 1912 in Iowa
Buried: June 1, 1913 Father: John C. Rollette (IL) Mother: Gertrude Mardis

Rhoads, Eldora Taylor (Book 2A Page 424 Monroe County)
Died: October 21, 1913 Aged: 29y 5m 11d Born: April 25, 1885 in Virginia
Buried: October 25, 1913 Father: John Taylor (VA) Mother: Carry Cozzins
Reasby, Mary (Book 2B Page 8 Monroe County)
Died: August 13, 1914 Aged: 5m Born: March 13, 1914 in Iowa
Buried: August 15, 1914 Father: Noah Reasby (VA) Mother: Unnamed
Roberts, Lenard (Book 2B Page 139 Monroe County)
Died: September 20, 1916 Aged: 66y Born: Virginia Buried: October 4, 1916
Father: Unknown (VA) Mother: Millie Fergus
Reeves, Ella (Book 2B Page 144 Monroe County)
Died: October 1, 1916 Aged: 37y Born: Buxton, Iowa Buried: October 2, 1916
Father: A. Laymans (WVA) Mother: Ella Laymans
Reeves, Chas. Edward (Book 2B Page 149 Monroe County)
Died: November 21, 1916 Aged: 18y 1m 5d Born: October 16, 1898 in Iowa
Buried: November 23, 1916 Father: William H. Reeves (VA) Mother: Ella Logoms
Reeves, Peter (Book 2B Page 195 Monroe County)
Died: September 28, 1917 Aged: 67y Born: 1850 in Virginia
Buried: October 2, 1917 Father: Not Given Mother: Not Given
Ross, Coy Jackson (1906- 1911 Mahaska County)
Died: October 29, 1909 Aged: Not Given Born: February 3, 1806 in Virginia
Buried: Not Given Father: Not Given Mother: Not Given

S:

Snell, William
Died: February 15, 1912 Aged: abt 70 years Born: Not Given
Buried: February 17, 1912 Father: Not Given Mother: Not Given
Shelton, Orvall S. (Book 2A Page 5 Monroe County)
Died: July 22, 1906 Aged: 27d Born: June 26, 1906 in Iowa
Buried: July 24, 1906 Father: Richard Shelton (TN) Mother: Mattie Holmes
Smith, John H. (Book 2A Page 9 Monroe County)
Died: August 21, 1906 Aged: 56y 2m 21d Born: June 5, 1850 in Missouri
Buried: August 24, 1906 Father: John H. Smith Mother: Elizabeth Smith
Sorrell, Unnamed (Book 2A Page 37 Monroe County)
Died: December 5, 1906 Stillborn Born: December 5, 1906 Buried: December 6, 1906
Father: Geo. Sorrell (VA) Mother: Liza Diza
Scales, Raman (Book 2A Page 45 Monroe County)
Died: January 20, 1907 Aged: 2y 6m Born: July 18, 1904 in Iowa
Buried: January 22, 1907 Father: Robt. Scales (NC) Mother: Bettie Runnels
Shepherd, Willie C. (Book 2A Page 45 Monroe County)
Died: January 10, 1907 Aged: 8m Born: May 8, 1906 in Iowa
Buried: January 12, 1907 Father: Wm. J. Shepherd (GA) Mother: Mary L. Martin
Smith, Alonda (Book 2A Page 46 Monroe County)
Died: January 25, 1907 Aged: 6m 2d Born: July 27, 1906 in Iowa
Buried: January 27, 1907 Father: A.L. Smith (AL) Mother: Marion Miller

Southall, Wm. (Book 2A Page 52 Monroe County)
Died; February 13, 1907 Aged: 46y Born: Virginia Buried: February 14, 1907
Father: Not Given (VA) Mother: Not Given

Smith, Unnamed (Book 2A Page 90 Monroe County)
Died: August 19, 1907 Aged: 1m 5d Born: July 14, 1907
Buried: August 20, 1907 Father: J.E. Smith (VA) Mother: Jane Welch

Seales, Robert (Book 2A Page 94 Monroe County)
Died: September 22, 1907 Aged: 42y Born: North Carolina
Buried: September 24, 1907 Father: Unnamed Anderson (NC) Mother: Ann Hopper

Smith, Sam (Book 2A Page 190 Monroe County)
Died: April 20, 1909 Aged: abt 95y Born: Not Given
Buried: April 24, 1909 Father: Wiley Smith Mother: Not Given

Smith, Infant (Book 2A Page 257 Monroe County)
Died: April 2, 1911 Aged: Not Given Born: January 1910
Buried: April 3, 1911 Father: Oscar Smith (VA) Mother: Not Given

Shades, James (Book 2A Page 267 Monroe County)
Died: June 4, 1911 Aged: 43y 6m 2d Born: January 2, 1868 in North Carolina
Buried: June 6, 1911 Father: Robert Shades (NC) Mother: Minerva Shades

Skipworth, William I. (Book 2A Page 348 Monroe County)
Died: August 25, 1912 Aged: 28y Born: August 24, 1884 in Virginia
Buried: August 28, 1912 Father: Iscum Skipwoth (VA) Mother: Ophelia Wellington

Buxton High School. (Monroe County Historical Museum.)

Sedlock, Infant (Book 2A Page 365 Monroe County)
Died: December 6, 1912 Stillborn Born: December 6, 1912
Buried: December 6, 1912 Father: George Sedlock (Austria) Mother: Mary Striffo
Sellers, Hattie (Book 2B Page 8 Monroe County)
Died: August 15, 1914 Aged: 52y 4m Born: April 15, 1862 in Wisconsin
Buried: August 17, 1914 Father: Dave Johnson Mother: Unknown
Slaughter, King (Book 2B Page 51 Monroe County)
Died: May 14, 1915 Aged: 54y 2m 4d Born: March 10, 1861 in Virginia
Buried: May 17, 1915 Father: Lee Slaughter (VA) Mother: Clara Barber
Southerland, Wm. M. (Book 2B Page 52 Monroe County)
Died: May 11, 1915 Aged: 46y 11m 9d Born: June 2, 1868 in Virginia
Buried: May 13, 1915 Father: Unknown Mother: Unknown
Stokes, George W. (Book 2B Page 85 Monroe County)
Died: December 6, 1915 Aged: 40y 1m Born: November 1875 in Virginia
Buried: December 8, 1915 Father: Unknown Mother: Unknown
Sandridge, Henry (Book 2B Page 119 Monroe County)
Died: May 14, 1916 Aged: abt 56y Born: abt 1860 in Virginia
Buried: May 17, 1916 Father: Unknown Mother: Unknown
Sikes/Soles, Mary Ann (Book 2B Page 190 Monroe County)
Died: August 31, 1917 Aged: 1y 3m 16d Born: May 15, 1916 in Iowa
Buried: September 1, 1917 Father: Rufus Sikes/ Soles (IN) Mother: Maude Benson
Sharp, Harry (Book 2B Page 222 Monroe County)
Died: February 4, 1918 Aged: 8m 11d Born: May 23, 1917 in Iowa
Buried: February 5, 1918 Father: Wm. Sharp Mother: Lucy Unnamed
Simms, D. S. (Book 2B Page 222 Monroe County)
Died: February 8, 1918 Aged: 1y 3m 7d (sic) Born: Virginia
Buried: February 10, 1918 Father: Not Given Mother: Not Given
Sykes, Maude (Book 2B Page 244 Monroe County)
Died: May 12, 1918 Age: 24y 11m 20d Born: May 22, 1893 in Macon, Missouri
Buried: May 15, 1918 Father: Unknown Mother: Unknown
Shepherd, Martha (Book 2B Page 251 Monroe County)
Died: June 21, 1918 Aged: abt 80y Born: Virginia
Buried: June 23, 1918 Father: Anthony Swann (VA) Mother: Unknown
Scales, Frank (Book 2B Page 266 Monroe County)
Died: September 5, 1918 Aged: 21y 8m 3d Born: January 2, 1897 in North Carolina
Buried: September 9, 1918 Father: R. Scales (NC) Mother: E. Renaelds (NC)
Smith, Dan (1906- 1911 Mahaska County)
Died: January 13, 1910 Aged: Not Given Born: February 13, 1890 in Iowa
Buried: Not Given Father: Not Given Mother: Not Given
Stewart, Martha (1906- 1911 Mahaska County)
Died: May 17, 1909 Aged: Not Given Born: March 10, 1882 in Iowa
Buried: Not Given Father: Not Given Mother: Not Given
Smith, Oscar (1911- 1915 Mahaska County)
Died: January 21, 1913 Aged: Not Given Born: September 15, 1889 in Missouri
Buried: Not Given Father: Not Given Mother: Not Given

Smith, Jalm Edd (June 1915- June 1919 Mahaska County)
Died: March 8, 1918 Aged: Not Given Born: July 16, 1867 in Virginia
Buried: Not Given Father: Not Given Mother: Not Given
Sebban, John Jr. (June 1915- June 1919 Mahaska County)
Died: October 12, 1916 Aged: Not Given Born: October 10, 1916 in Iowa
Buried: Not Given Father: Not Given Mother: Not Given

T:

Thompson, Carry (Book 2A Page 9 Monroe County)
Died: August 1, 1906 Aged: 36y Born: March 1870 in Alabama
Buried: August 3, 1906 Father: L. Washington (AL) Mother: America Towns
Taylor, Shelby M. (Book 2A Page 17 Monroe County)- Adopted
Died: September 7, 1906 Aged: 10y 8m Born: December 8, 1886 in Iowa
Buried: September 9, 1906 Father: John Taylor (IA) Mother: Cora A. Taylor
Tanks, James (Book 2A Page 32 Monroe County)
Died: November 28, 1906 Aged: 60y Born: Virginia
Buried: November 30, 1906 Father: Jerry Unnamed Mother: Bessie Tanks
Taylor, Unnamed (Book 2A Page 74 Monroe County)
Died: May 19, 1907 Aged: 12 hours Born: May 19, 1907 in Iowa
Buried: May 20, 1907 Father: Geo. Taylor Mother: Unnamed
Toliver, John Sr. (Book 2A Page 99 Monroe County)
Died: October 26, 1907 Aged: 57y 7m Born: March 1850 in Virginia
Buried: October 27, 1907 Father: Anderson Toliver (VA) Mother: Not Given
Thomas, Bessie (Book 2A Page 131 Monroe County)
Died: April 28, 1908 Aged: 47y Born: Missouri
Buried: May 1, 1918 Father: Unnamed Langhard (VA) Mother: Bessie Thomas
Thomas, Darlene (Book 2A Page 146 Monroe County)
Died: August 19, 1908 Aged: 8m 9d Born: December 10, 1907 in Iowa
Buried: August 20, 1908 Father: Jack Thomas (MO) Mother: Ellen Hunter
Tolson, Roy (Book 2A Page 165 Monroe County)
Died: December 9, 1908 Aged: 11y 9m Born: March 4 in Iowa
Buried: Not Given Father: Cornell G. Tolson (MO) Mother: Mollie Stubleton
Turner, Unnamed (Book 2A Page 208 Monore County)
Died: July 28, 1910 Aged: 6m Born: Iowa
Buried: July 30, 1910 Father: W.H. Turner (IA) Mother: J. Spears
Taylor, Matthew (Book 2A Page 228 Monroe County)
Died: November 8, 1910 Aged: abt 33y Born: North Carolina
Buried: November 13, 1910 Father: Not Given Mother: Not Given
Toran, Lorenzo (Book 2A Page 317 Monroe County)
Died: February 27, 1912 Aged: 2y 6m 7d Born: August 20, 1910 in Iowa
Buried: March 1, 1912 Father: Frank Toran (VA) Mother: Hozana James
Thomas, James (Book 2A Page 418 Monroe County)- Murdered
Died: September 14, 1913 Aged: Not Given Born: Louisiana
Buried: September 15, 1913 Father: Not Given Mother: Not Given

Turner, Eugene (Book 2B Page 15 Monroe County)
Died: October 7, 1914 Aged: 29y 4m 26d Born: May 11, 1885 in Alabama
Buried: October 10, 1914 Father: Charles Turner Mother: Unknown
Turner, Unnamed (Book 2B Page 65 Monroe County)
Died: August 6, 1915 Stillborn Born: August 6, 1915 in Iowa
Buried: August 7, 1915 Father: Howard Turner Mother: Leona Burds
Tolson, Fred (Book 2B Page 86 Monroe County)
Died: December 13, 1915 Aged: 26y 4m 19d Born: July 24, 1889 in Missouri
Buried: December 15, 1915 Father: Chas. F. Tolson (MO) Mother: Mary Stableton
Thomas, Henrietta (Book 2B Page 113 Monroe County)
Died: April 12, 1916 Aged: 52y 4m 0d Born: Decemebr 12, 1863 in Maryland
Buried: April 4, 1916 Father: W.H. Brown (MD) Mother: Martha A. Covey
Taylor, Sloan (Book 2B Page 160 Monroe County)- Murdered
Died: January 8, 1917 Aged: 22y 7m 0d Born: June 7, 1894 in Iowa
Buried: January 10, 1917 Father: W.M. Taylor Mother: Ella Allen
Thomas, Calvin (Book 2B Page 312 Monroe County)
Died: January 10, 1919 Aged: 12 hours Born: January 10, 1919 in Iowa
Buried: January 11, 1919 Father: Calvin Thomas (AL) Mother: Surena Bell (MO)
Tolliver, J.W. (1906- 1911 Mahaska County)
Died: March 19, 1908 Aged; Not Given Born: December 13, 1871 in Virginia
Buried: Not Given Father: Not Given Mother: Not Given
Tolson, Francis (June 1915- June 1919 Mahaska County)
Died: April 30, 1919 Aged: Not Given Born: November 19, 1918 in Iowa
Buried: Not Given Father: Not Given Mother: Not Given

V:

Vipond, Unnamed (Book 2B Page 196 Monroe County)
Died: September 27, 1917 Stillborn Born: September 27, 1917 in Iowa
Buried: September 27, 1917 Father: John Vipond (IA) Mother: Bertha Snooks

W:

West, Frank Jr.
Died: April 9, 1923 Aged: 4m 2d Born: Not Given
Buried: April 11, 1923 Father: Not Given Mother: Not Given
Wesley, Lionel
Died: April 18, 1902 Aged: 1y 11m Born: Buxton Iowa
Buried: Not Given Father: Not Given Mother: Not Given
Walker, George Washington
Died: June 16, 1903 Aged: 37y 4m 1d Born: Alabama Co., Virginia
Buried: Not Given Father: Not Given Mother: Not Given
Walker, John (Garland Van Arkel Langkamp Funeral Home- Mahaska County)
Died: May 25, 1923 Aged: 70y Born: Virginia
Buried: Not Given Father: Not Given Mother: Not Given

Wood, Mary W. (Book 2A Page 11 Monroe County)
Died: August 23, 1906 Aged: 71y 7m 19d Born: February 6, 1835 in Virginia
Buried: August 25, 1906 Father: Unnamed Cobbs (VA) Mother: Fanny Cobbs
Wheels, Dora (Book 2A Page 18 Monroe County)
Died: September 15, 1906 Aged: 21y Born: November in Iowa
Buried: September 17, 1906 Father: Jas. Wheels (VA) Mother: Amanda Macha
Williams, Unnamed (Book 2A Page 18 Monroe County)
Died: September 29, 1906 Stillborn Born: September 29, 1906 in Iowa
Buried: September 29, 1906 Father: J.C. Williams (IA) Mother: Lottie Wright
Williams, Beatrice (Book 2A Page 27 Monroe County)
Died: October 5, 1906 Aged: 19y Born: January 1885 in Alabama
Buried: October 6, 1906 Father: Unnamed Milden Mother: Pricilla Milden
Williams, Emma (Book 2A Page 46 Monroe County)
Died: January 12, 1907 Aged: 35y Born: September 25, 1872 in Virginia
Buried: January 14, 1907 Father: Unnamed Mother: Susan Harris
Wilson, Cornelius (Book 2A Page 47 Monroe County)
Died: January 7, 1907 Aged: 2y 10d Born: March 19, 1904 in Iowa
Buried: January 9, 1907 Father: Jacob Wilson (VA) Mother: Lizzie Logan
Williams, Charles (Book 2A Page 62 Monroe County)
Died: March 5, 1907 Aged: 55y 5d Born: March 1, 1852 in Kentucky
Buried: March 7, 1907 Father: Charlie Williams Mother: Unnamed
Wilson, Jerry (Book 2A Page 62 Monroe County)
Died: March 24, 1907 Aged: 66y Born: 1841 in Virginia
Buried: March 25, 1907 Father: Jerry Wilson (VA) Mother: Ella Wilson
Winston, Robert (Book 2A Page 67 Monroe County)
Died: April 18, 1907 Aged: 44y 5m 5d Born: October 15 in Virginia
Buried: April 21, 1907 Father: Henry Winston (VA) Mother: Nancy Ping
Wood, Alpha L.O. (Book 2A Page 68 Monroe County)
Died: April 5, 1907 Aged: 1y 7m 14d Born: August 22, 1905 in Iowa
Buried: April 7, 1907 Father: B.M. Wood (VA) Mother: Bessie Taylor
Williams, Celia (Book 2A Page 85 Monroe County)
Died: July 4, 1907 Aged: 31y 7m 11d Born: January 15, 1876 in Virginia
Buried: July 6, 1907 Father: Orin Gibson (VA) Mother: Anna Gibson
Watkins, Samie (Book 2A Page 95 Monroe County)
Died: September 2, 1907 Aged: 26y 1m 17d Born: July 14, 1881 in Virginia
Buried: September 29, 1907 Father: Sam'l Watkins (VA) Mother: L. Douglas
Watkins, W.J. (Book 2A Page 95 Monroe County)
Died: September 28, 1907 Aged: 8m 9d Born: December 19, 1906 in Iowa
Buried: September 29, 1907 Father: J.A. Watkins (VA) Mother: Mary Sanders
Woodfolk, Vera Ann (Book 2A Page 95 Monroe County)
Died: September 27, 1907 Aged: 18y 3m 27d Born: May 30, 1889 in Iowa
Buried: September 29, 1907 Father: Rob't Woodfolk (VA) Mother: Mary Flemmens
Willis, George (Book 2A Page 100 Monroe County)
Died: October 28, 1907 Aged: 32y 8d Born: October 20, 1875 in Virginia
Buried: November 1, 1907 Father: Randolph Willis (VA) Mother: Lucy Carter

Walker, Lewis (Book 2A Page 104 Monroe County)
Died: November 16, 1907 Aged: 1y 10m 11d Born: January 8, 1906 in Iowa
Buried: November 19, 1907 Father: Rob't L. Walker (VA) Mother: Mary J. Rhodes
Willis, George A. (Book 2A Page 129 Monroe County)
Died: March 5, 1908 Aged: 19y 5m 13d Born: August 18, 1889 in Virginia
Buried: March 8, 1908 Father: Unnamed Mother: Unnamed Tyler
Woodfork, Robert (Book 2A Page 138 Monroe County)
Died: June 25, 1908 Aged: 40y Born: Virginia
Buried: June 29, 1908 Father: Not Given Mother: Nellie Woodfork
Webster, Robert (Book 2A Page 142 Monroe County)
Died: July 29, 1908 Aged: 52y Born: 1856 Buried: August 2, 1908
Father: Not Given Mother: Not Given
Wesley, Sarah (Book 2A Page 160 Monroe County)
Died: November 20, 1908 Aged: 42y 9m 12d Born: February 8, 1866 in Virginia
Buried: November 22, 1908 Father: Wm. Kinney (VA) Mother: Anne Kinney
Watkins, B. (Book 2A Page 166 Monroe County)
Died: December 18, 1908 Aged: 23y 6m 18d Born: June 15, 1885 in Iowa
Buried: December 21, 1908 Father: Unnamed Watkins (VA) Mother: Louisa Unnamed
Williams, John M. (Book 2A Page 191 Monroe County)
Died: April 22, 1909 Aged: abt 55y Born: Not Given
Buried: April 23, 1909 Father: Not Given Mother: Not Given
Wilson, Samuel (Book 2A Page 245 Monroe County)
Died: February 18, 1911 Aged: 62y 7m 10d Born: August 8, 1849 in Virginia
Buried: February 21, 1911 Father: Samuel Wilson (VA) Mother: Ellen Unnamed
Woodford, George (Book 2A Page 263 Monroe County)
Died: May 8, 1911 Aged: 22y 4m 5d Born: February 3, 1889 in Iowa
Buried: May 11, 1911 Father: Isaac C. Woodford (VA) Mother: Anna Stribling
White, Bula (Book 2A Page 281 Monroe County)
Died: August 14, 1911 Aged: 3m Born: May 14, 1911 in Iowa
Buried: August 15, 1911 Father: Unknown Mother: Bula White
Wilson, Bettie (Book 2A Page 311 Monroe County)
Died: January 26, 1912 Aged: 66y Born: Virginia
Buried: Not Given Father: Reuben Gaines (VA) Mother: Mariar Gaines
Woods, Marry (Book 2A Page 318 Monroe County)
Died: February 18, 1912 Aged: 5y 1m 10d Born: December 8, 1906 in Iowa
Buried: February 21, 1912 Father: Frank Woods (TN) Mother: Dollie Shepard
White, Dunn (Book 2A Page 344 Monroe County)
Died: July 4, 1912 Aged: abt 65y Born: Virginia
Buried: July 6, 1912 Father: Not Given Mother: Not Given
Weston, John (Book 2A Page 431 Monroe County)
Died: November 11, 1913 Aged: 83y 1m 17d Born: December 25, 1829 in North Carolina
Buried: November 13, 1913 Father: Jim Hampton (NC) Mother: Isabella Weston
Williams, Jno. (Book 2A Page 456 Monroe County)
Died: March 18, 1914 Aged: abt 27y Born: Virginia
Buried: March 21, 1914 Father: John Williams (VA) Mother: Eveline Young

Gaines plot in Buxton Cemetery, before cleaning in 2002. See page 108-09. (Dickey collection.)

Ward, Robert (Book 2A Page 460 Monroe County)
Died: April 25, 1914 Aged: 49y 2m 15d Born: February 10, 1865 in North Carolina
Buried: April 27, 1914 Father: Robert Ward (NC) Mother: Martha Thompson
Watson, Susie (Book 2A Page 460 Monroe County)
Died: April 5, 1914 Aged: 16y 6m 4d Born: October 1, 1898 in Virginia
Buried: April 7, 1914 Father: C.G. Watson (VA) Mother: Rosa Jackson
Watkins, Thomas (Book 2A Page 467 Monroe County)
Died: May 5, 1914 Aged: 42y 17d Born: April 19, 1872 in Virginia
Buried: May 7, 1914 Father: Unknown Mother: Unknown
Williams, Sidney (Book 2B Page 4 Monroe County)
Died: July 28, 1914 Aged: 61y Born: Virginia
Buried: July 30, 1914 Father: Unknown Mother: Unknown
Walker, Pauline (Book 2B Page 43 Monroe County)
Died: March 31, 1915 Aged: 41y 1m 3d Born: February 28, 1874 in Virginia
Buried: April 3, 1915 Father: Peter Moore (VA) Mother: Susan Cheathem
Winston, Lucy (Book 2B Page 53 Monroe County)
Died: May 6, 1915 Aged: 87y 10m 26d Born: June 10, 1827 in Virginia
Buried: May 9, 1915 Father: Unknown Mother: Unknown

West, Lee Andrew (Book 2B Page 120 Monroe County)
Died: May 25, 1916 Aged: 38y 7m 5d Born: October 20, 1877 in Tennessee
Buried: May 28, 1916 Father: Not Given Mother: Not Given
Ward, Bell (Book 2B Page 145 Monroe County)
Died: October 2, 1916 Aged: abt 49y Born: Not Given
Buried: October 5, 1916 Father: Not Given Mother: Unnamed Higby
Welch, Ellen (Book 2B Page 153 Monroe County)
Died: December 28, 1916 Aged: 79y 10m 14d Born: February 14, 1837 in Missouri
Buried: December 29, 1916 Father: Samuel Tucker (MO) Mother: Maria Unnamed
Woodley, Leatha (Book 2B Page 336 Monroe County)
Died: May 6, 1919 Aged: 23y 10m 3d Born: July 3, 1895 in Alabama
Buried: Not Given Father: Frank Jackson (MS) Mother: Dora Chambers
Williams, Earl (1906-1911 Mahaska County)
Died: April 19, 1911 Aged: Not Given
Born: March 31, 1911 in Iowa
Buried: Not Given Father: Not Given
Mother: Not Given
Walker, Charles (1911- 1915 Mahaska County)
Died: July 18, 1913 Aged: Not Given
Born: 1868 in Virginia
Buried: Not Given Father: Not Given
Mother: Not Given
Wesley, James Edman (1911- 1915 Mahaska County)
Died: February 22, 1913 Aged: Not Given Born: February 2, 1861 in Virginia
Buried: Not Given Father: Not Given
Mother: Not Given

Buxton Cemetery sign listing burials. (Michael W. Lemberger)

Y

Young, Unnamed (Book 2A Page 411 Monroe County)
Died: August 9, 1913 Aged: 1d Born: August 8, 1913 in Iowa
Buried: August 10, 1913 Father: Guss Young (MO) Mother: Nora Kelsy
Young, Augusta (Book 2B Page 160 Monroe County)
Died: January 7, 1917 Aged: 41y 5m 1d Born: August 6, 1875
Buried: January 9, 1917 Father: Unreadable (VA) Mother: Marriland
Young, Edward C. (Book 2B Page 161 Monroe County)
Died: January 28, 1917 Aged: 1y 1d Born: January 27, 1916 in Iowa
Buried: January 30, 1917 Father: Augusta Young (MO) Mother: Maria Kelsa

Known Burials at Buxton Cemetery

This alphabetical listing of known burials at Buxton Cemetery has been compiled from a survey of stones in the cemetery, augmented with other sources including county death records, WPA surveys, and family information. Records are not always complete, and spellings vary. Small photos of individual stones have been placed near the listing of the deceased.

Abington, Jane. Born Dec. 1, 1875. Died March 2, 1916. Age 40 y 3m 1 d. Burial date March 6, 1916.

Allen, Infant. Born March 20, 1909. Died April 27, 1909. Age 27 d. Burial date April 29, 1909

Allen, John Henry. Born March ?, ? Died June 19, 1914. Age 59 y. Burial date June 21, 1914.

Allen, Unnamed. Died Feb. 13, 1907. Age 78y. Burial date Feb. 15, 1907.

Allen, Unnamed. Born Dec. 5, 1907. Burial date Dec. 6, 1907.

Ampey, Dorothy M. Born Feb. 1, 1903. Died Dec. 1, 1906. Age 3 y 10 m. Burial date Dec. 3, 1906.

Anderson, B.T./ O.T. No dates available. Civil War veteran.

Anderson, Gertrude. Born Feb. 19, 1906. Died Sept. 14, 1906. Age 6 m 26 d. Burial date Sept. 17, 1906.

Anderson, Roma. Born Jan. 1, 1905. Died June 19, 1909. Age 4 y 11 m 9 d. Burial date June 21, 1909.

Arthur, Sally May. Born July 2, 1905. Died July 8, 1907. Age 2 y 6 d. Burial date July 9, 1907.

Baird, Stella E. Born July 30, 1897. Died Sept. 21, 1906. Age 9 y 1 m 22 d. Burial date Sept. 24, 1906.

Baker, King. Born Sept. 8, 1912. Age about 68 yrs. Burial date Sept. 9, 1912.

Baker, Kittie. Died March 16, 1907. Age 82y. Burial date March 18, 1907.

Baker, Marie C. Born March 18, 1906. Died Dec. 30, 1907. Age 9 m 12 d. Burial date Jan. 1, 1908.

Baker, Minnie (Fields).* Born Sept. 18, 1873. Died June 12, 1919.

Baker, Simmon. Died Aug. 27, 1913. Age 91y. Burial date Aug. 29, 1913.

Bales, Essie May. Born May 17, ? Died Feb. 21, 1915. Age 19 y 9 m 4 d. Burial date Feb. 25, 1915.

Banner, Mattie. Born Aug. 10, 1856. Died Nov. 1, 1908. Burial date Nov. 2, 1908.

Banks, George. No dates available. Source: WPA.

Barbee, Infant. Born Nov. 15, 1907. Died Nov. 15, 1907. Stillborn. Burial date Nov. 16, 1907.

Barber, Bertha.* Born Dec. 19, 1892. Died March 12, 1917.

Bates, Henry Clifford. Born Dec. 16, 1888. Died Sept. 28, 1912. Age 23 y 9 m 12 d. Burial date Oct. 1, 1912.

Bates, Robert Douglass. Born July 18, 1819. Died Dec. 4, 1918. Age 99 y 4 m 17 d. Burial date Dec. 7, 1918.

Beadle, Charles. Died Feb. 24, 1915. Age 43y 11 m 20 d. Burial date Feb. 26, 1915.

Bennett, Zelma Marie. Born Sept. 19, 1908. Died April 25, 1909. Age 7 m 6 d. Burial date April 27, 1909.

Berger, Roxie. Born Sept. 5, 1883. Died Feb. 23, 1907. Age 24 y 6 m 18 d. Burial date Feb. 25, 1907.

Berges, Howard. Born July 4, 1879. Died Jan. 13, 1907. Age 27 y. Burial date Jan. 16, 1907.

Bergstrom, Katrina. Born Jan. 15, 1836. Died Aug. 16, 1917. Age 81 y 7 m 1 d. Burial date Aug. 19, 1917.

Bingham, Rebecca. (Mrs. Steward Bingham.) Born Dec. 22, 1864. Died April 2, 1918. Age 53 y 3 m 11 d. Burial date April 5, 1918. Source: WPA

Blackman, Rena. Died Dec. 29, 1912. Age about 57 yrs. Burial date Jan. 1, 1913.

Blainey, Ardell J. Born Oct. 13, 1908. Died Nov. 6, 1908. Age 28 d. Burial date Nov. 7, 1908.

Blainey, Laura V. Mrs. Born May 4, 1854. Died March 4, 1912. Age 58 y 10 m. Burial date March 7, 1912. (WPA lists birth date as 1851.)

Blainey, Mally (Mallie). Born July 15, 1888. Died Oct. 3, 1906. Age 18 y 2 m 14 d. Burial date Oct. 4, 1906. (WPA lists death date as 1907.)

Blakey, Georgia Alice. Died May 25, 1903. Age 3 y 11 m 23 d.

Bolden, Bert. Born March 28, 1906. Died Nov. 24, 1916. Age 10 y 7 m 26 d. Burial date Nov. 25, 1916.

Booker, Eliza. Died March 18, 1912. Age about 62 yrs. Burial date March 21, 1912.

Booker, Herman. Born March 15, 1910. Died June 27, 1911. Age 1 y 3 m 12 d. Burial date June 28, 1911.

Boston, William.* Born September 24, 1883. Died Sept. 24, 1910.

Boston, Wm. M. Born May 31, 1906. Died Jan. 9, 1907. Age 7 m 8 d. Burial date Jan. 11, 1907.

Bowers, Joe. Born March 22 1880. Died Jan. 22, 1907. Age 20 y 10 m 1 d. Burial date Jan. 25, 1907.

Bowles, Alice (Boles). Born March 15, 1871. Died Aug. 31, 1906. Age 35 y 6 m 15 d. Burial date Sept. 2, 1906. (WPA lists birth date as 1872.)

Braxton, Cora E. Died May 11, 1908. Age 18 y. Burial date May 14, 1908.

Brinker, Bengiman Ernest. Born April 2, 1911. Died July 30, 1913. Age 2 y 3 m 23 d. Burial date Aug. 2, 1913.

Brooks, Annie Elisabeth. Born March 12, 1905. Died Aug. 5, 1914. Age 9 y 4 m 24 d. Burial date Aug. 6, 1914.

Above and right: Panorama of the Gaines plot, 2007. (Michael W. Lemberger)

Brooks, George W. Born April 23, 1870. Died Oct. 11, 1917. Age 47 y 5 m 18 d. Burial date Oct. 16, 1917.

Brooks, James. Born April 5, 1901. Died July 30, 1914. Age 13 y 3 m 25 d. Burial date Aug. 1, 1914.

Brown, Electra. Born Feb. 28, 1889. Died Nov. 15, 1906. Age 18 y 8 m 7 d. Burial date Nov. 15, 1906.

Brown, Hattie. Born Aug. 5, 1869. Died Aug. 17, 1918. Age 49 y 12 d.

Brown, Jacob. Born 1830. Died April 8, 1904. Age 74 y. (Source of birth date WPA.)

Brown, Jennie. "Wife" Died Sept. 15, 1905. Age 68 y. (Wife of Jacob: WPA.)

Brown, John. Died Sept. 18, 1907. Age 29 y. Burial date Sept. 23, 1907.

Brown, Malcenia. Born Jan. 10, 1912. Died Oct. 13, 1913. Age 9m 2 d. (sic) Burial date Oct. 14, 1913.

Brown, Mary. Born Jan. 17, 1869. Died May 20, 1916. Age 47 y 4 m 3 d. Burial date May 22, 1916.

Bryant, Hannah. Died Nov. 15, 1908. Age 73 y. Burial date Nov. 18, 1908.

Bryson, Carl. Born Feb. 6, 1901. Died Aug. 10, 1914. Age 13 y 6 m 4 d. Burial date Aug. 12, 1914.

Bryson, Maggie. Born April 1, ? Died Jan. 31, 1911. Age 35 y 10 m 1 d. Burial date Feb. 2, 1911.

Burgess, Minta (Middie). Born March 1849. Died June 29, 1907. Age 59 y 3 m. Burial date June 30, 1907. (Source: WPA.)

Burgess, Roxa (Roxsa). Born Sept. 5, 1883. Died May 21, 1907.

Burkett, Unnamed. Born Sept. 1906. Died Sept. 25, 1906. Burial date Sept. 25, 1906.

Burkey, John Henry. Died Dec. 23, 1903. Age 8 y 3 m.

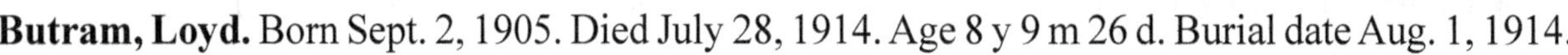

Butram, Loyd. Born Sept. 2, 1905. Died July 28, 1914. Age 8 y 9 m 26 d. Burial date Aug. 1, 1914.

Buttram, Landon. Born May 27, 1901. Died May 8, 1914. Age 13 y 11 m 19 d. Burial date May 10, 1914.

Byers, Loyd. Born Sept. 5, 1888. Died May 21, 1914. Age 26 y 2 m 16 d. Burial date May 23, 1914.

Cannedy, John T. Born Jan. 31, 1853. Died July 29, 1907. Age 54 y 6 m 29 d. Burial date July 31, 1907.

Carell, Henry. Born Dec. 10, ? Died March 13, 1907. Age 18 y. Burial date March 16, 1907.

Carey, Bettie. Died Sept. 11, 1910. Age 50 y. Burial date Sept. 13, 1910.

Carey, Mary F. Born Feb. 2, 1879. Died Nov. 22, 1911. Age 32 y 9 m. Burial date Nov. 24, 1911.

Carpenter, Mildred A. Died Nov. 29, 1910. Age 44 y 1 m 21 d. Burial date Dec. 1, 1910.

Carpenter, Winifred. Born Feb. 19, 1919. Died March 1, 1919. Age 10 d. Burial date March 2, 1919.

Carr, Dorthy May. Born July 16, 1911. Died Nov. 19, 1911. Age 5 m 3 d. Burial date Nov. 21, 1911.

Carr, John M. Died March 11, 1919. Age about 64 yrs. Burial date March 13, 1919.

Carr, Mary. Born Feb. 1, 1877. Died Feb. 12, 1915. Age 38 y 12 d. Burial date Feb. 15, 1915.

Carson, James. Died Feb. 7, 1913. Age 38 y. Burial date Feb. 10, 1913.

Carter, Chas. Nelson. Born Oct. 15, 1850. Died Feb. 16, 1915. Age 64 y 4 m 1 d. Burial date Feb. 18, 1915.

Carter, George Washington. Born Sept. 19, 1859. Died April 19, 1918. Age 58 y 7 m. Burial date April 22, 1918.

Carter, Jennie. Born March 1870. Died June 17, 1915. Age 45 y 3 m. Burial date June 21, 1915.

Carter, Jesteene. Born Oct. 1, 1887. Died Jan. 20, 1912. Age 22 y 3 m 20 d. Burial date Jan. 23, 1912.

Carter, Pauline L. Born Sept. 16, 1882. Died Sept. 26, 1909.

Carter, S.J. Born July 30, 1861. Died June 30, 1907. Age 46 y 11 m. Burial date July 2, 1907.

Carter, William Edward. Born Nov. 18, 1918. Died March 19, 1919. Age 4 m 1 d. Burial date March 20, 1919.

Casey, Geo. M. Born June 1, 1850. Died June 14, 1919. Age 69 y 13 d. Burial date June 17, 1919.

Chambers, Griffin. Died Feb. 18, 1916.

Chambers, Griffith. Born Jan. 12, 1871. Died March 3, 1915. Age 44 y 1 m 19 d. Burial date March 4, 1915.

Chatman, Mary Miller. Died Oct. 26, 1911. Age 77 y. Burial date Oct. 28, 1911.

Cheatham, Eliza. Died Feb. 19, 1912. Age 79 y. Burial date Feb. 22, 1912.

Cheffee, Susan Lawson.* Born May 13, 1885. Died Sept. 30, 1910.

Clark, Flossie. Born Sept. 15, 1915. Died Feb. 24, 1916. Age 5 m 9 d. Burial date Feb. 26, 1916.

Clinton, James C. Born June 28, 1906. Died Aug. 20, 1907. Age 1 y 1 m 20 d. Burial date Aug. 20, 1907.

Cobb, Robert. Died Nov.19, 1911. Age 54 y. Burial date Nov. 21, 1911

Coleman, Delia E. Born Nov. 17, 1869. Died Dec. 3, 1908. Age 39 y 16 d. Burial date Dec. 6, 1908.

Compostine, Infant. Born Nov. 25, 1910. Died Nov. 25, 1910. Stillborn. Burial date Nov. 25, 1910.

Compton, James. Died Oct. 25, 1911. Age 40 y. Burial date Oct. 27, 1911.

Conwell, Mandy. Died July 23, 1906. Age 40 y. Burial date July 25, 1906.

Cook, Eliz. Born April 8, 1889. Died Nov. 1, 1906. Age 17 y. Burial date Nov. 3, 1906.

Crank, Mary S. Born Oct. 10, 1868. Died Oct. 10, 1912. Age 44 y. Burial date Oct. 13, 1912.

Croft, Infant. Born June 30, 1911. Died June 30, 1911. Stillborn. Burial date July 1, 1911.

Cronk, B.F. Mrs. Died Oct. 1912.

Cross, August. Born Aug. 6, 1911. Died Jan. 8, 1912. Age 4 m. Burial date Jan. 9, 1912.

Cross,Augusta. Born Aug. 6, 1911. Died Sept. 15, 1911. Age 1 m 12 d. Burial date Sept. 16, 1911.

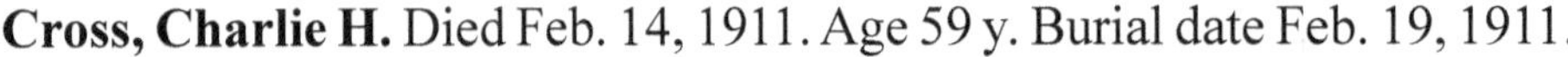

Cross, Charlie H. Died Feb. 14, 1911. Age 59 y. Burial date Feb. 19, 1911.

Crowder, Charles William. Born Feb. 14, 1909. Died Oct. 4, 1918. Age 9 y 7 m 20 d. Burial date Oct. 4, 1918.

Cunningham, Unnamed. Born Aug. 30, 1906. Died Sept. 1, 1906. Age 3 d. Burial date Sept. 2, 1906.

Cunningham,Clarence Mrs. Died Sept. 14, 1906. Age 35 y. Burial date Sept. 18, 1906.

Curtis, Priscilla. Born 1858. Died March 12, 1916. Age 58 y. Burial date March 15, 1916.

Davenport, Henry. Died March 25, 1911. Age about 42 yrs. Burial date March 29, 1911.

Davis, Millie. Died May 1, 1912. Age about 39 yrs. Burial date May 3, 1912.

Deering, Infant. Born April 23, 1911. Died May 23, 1911. Age 28 d. Burial date May 23, 1911.

DeSleet, Nella G. Born June 20, 1896. Died May 4, 1916. Age 19 y 10 m 14 d. Burial date May 6, 1916.

DeVorce, Infant. Died Jan. 5, 1908. Stillborn. Burial date Jan. 5, 1908.

Dickson, Fanny. Born April 2, 1882. Died July 11, 1907. Age 25 y 3 m 9 d. Burial date July 12, 1907.

Dickson, Theodor. Born March 13, 1906. Died Jan. 7, 1907. Age 10 m 25 d. Burial date Jan. 9, 1907

Downs, Edward J. Died Jan. 25, 1914. Age about 37 yrs. Burial date Jan. 27, 1914.

Doyle, Eliza. Born March 6, 1907. Died March 6, 1907. Burial date March 6, 1907.

Doyle, Louie. Born Nov. 24, 1908. Died Jan. 27, 1909. Burial date Jan. 28, 1909.

Dyke, Infant. Born April 12, 1918. Died April 23, 1918. Age 12 d. Burial date April 23, 1918.

Elligan, Infant. Born April 15, 1908. Died April 25, 1908. Age 10 d. Burial date April 26, 1908.

Ellis, James T. Born June 29, 1840. Died Nov. 4, 1913. Age 73y 4 m 25 d. Burial date Nov. 6, 1913.

Ewing, Infant. Born April 9, 1912. Died April 9, 1912. Stillborn. Burial date April 10, 1912.

Ewing, Lucy Luiza. Born April 11, 1865. Died March 9, 1915. Age 49 y l0 m 26 d. Burial date March 11, 1915.

Fargay, Fred. Born July 28, 1874. Died May 26, 1918. Age 43 y 9 m 28 d. Burial date May 30, 1918.

Fergeson, Lewis. Born Dec.25, ? Died Jan. 3, 1912. Age 73 y 9 d. Burial date Jan. 5, 1912.

Fields, Hermis.* Born July 30, 1904. Died June 24, 1907.

Floyd, Ervin. Born March 10, 1857. Died Oct. 4, 1907. Age 50 y 7 m 24 d. Burial date Oct. 6, 1907.

Gaines, Moses. Born Aug. 28, 1855. Died May 12, 1918. Age 62 y 8 m 15 d. Burial date May 14, 1918.

Gaines, Parents of Reuben. No data available.

Gaines, Reuben. Died Oct. 7, 1922. Age 62 y 9 m 26 d.

Gardon, Emma Lee. Born Aug. 10, 1895. Died June 14, 1915. Age 19 y 10 m 4 d. Burial date June 16, 1915.

Garnett, Emery. Born Feb. 22, 1913. Died. March 9, 1913. Age 15 d. Burial date March 10, 1913.

Garnett, Joe Jr. Born June 28, 1916. Died Feb. 23, 1918. Age 1 y 7 m 25 d. Burial date Feb. 26, 1918.

Garrett, Beatrice Bernice. Born July 14, 1914. Died March 9, 1918. Age 3 y 7 m 23 d. Burial date March 10, 1918.

Garrett, Warren Andrew. Born Feb. 2, 1918. Died March 21, 1918. Age l m 19 d. Burial date March 23, 1918.

Gibbons, William E. Born July 21, 1917. Died Sept. 27, 1917. Age 2 m 6 d. Burial date Sept. 18, 1917.

Glass, Infant. Born April 7, 1907. Died Aug. 3, 1907. Age 4 m 27 d. Burial date Aug. 4, 1907.

Glass, Syvanis. Born April 11, 1896. Died Sept. 8, 1906. Age 4 m 28 d. Burial date Sept. 9, 1906.

Gowin, James. Died July 29, 1914. Age about 55 yrs. Burial date July 31, 1914.

Granison, Meridith. Born March 14,1854. Died Aug. 28, 1916. Age 62y 8 m 14 d. Burial date Aug. 31, 1916.

Graves, Dorothy. Born March 12, 1911. Died Dec. 19, 1911. Age 9 m 5 d. Burial date Dec. 20, 1911.

Graves, Elsie M. Born April 20, 1894. Died Jan. 25, 1913. Age 19 y 9 m 5 d. Burial date Jan. 27, 1913.

Graves, George. Died 1909.

Graves, Jessie. Born April 24, 1911. Died Aug. 10, 1914. Age 3 y 3 m 17 d. Burial date Aug. 10, 1914.

Graves, John H. Died Jan. 27, 1914. Age 52 y. Burial date Jan. 30, 1914.

Graves, John W. Born June 12, 1902. Died July 29, 1914. Age 12 y 1 m 17 d. Burial date Aug. 1, 1914.

Graves, Jordon. Died Feb. 1, 1902. Age about 39 yrs.

Graves, Josie. Born June 8, 1899. Died Aug. 10, 1914. Age 15 y 2 m 2 d. Burial date Aug. 11, 1914.

Graves, Lee. Born April 25, 1907. Died April 25, 1907. Stillborn. Burial date April 26, 1907.

Graves, Paul. Born Nov. 5, 1909. Died Aug. 9, 1914. Age 5 y 9 m 4 d. Burial date Aug. 9, 1914.

Graves, Thelma. Born Nov. 7, 1912. Died Aug. 5, 1914. Age 1 y 8 m 29 d. Burial date Aug. 6, 1914.

Green, Ada Mrs. Died Jan. 26, 1914. Age 39 y. Burial date Jan. 28, 1914.

Green, Estella. Born March 11, 1907. Died March 20, 1908. Age l y 9 m. Burial date March 22, 1908.

Grevious, Jessie W. Born Sept. 5, 1905. Died Jan. 22, 1907. Age l y 5 m. Burial date Jan. 24, 1907.

Griggs, John. Born March 4, 1855. Died May 23, 1919. Age 64 y 2 m 19 d. Burial date May 24, 1919.

Grimes, Levi. Born Feb. 23, 1895. Died Feb. 22, 1907. Age 11 y 11 m 27 d. Burial date Feb. 24, 1907.

Guy, Eva A. Mrs. Born Nov. 5, 1883. Died Oct. 10, 1910. Age 26 y 11 m 5 d. Burial date Oct. 13, 1910.

Hackett, Minnie. Born Aug. 2, 1893. Died Aug. 8, 1906. Age 13 y 4 d. Burial date Aug. 8, 1906.

Hale, Polly. Born June 1866. Died Oct. 19, 1906. Age 40 y. Burial date Oct. 22, 1906.

Hanley, Child. Born Nov. 18, 1904. Died Nov. 28, 1907. Age 3 y 10 d. Burial date Nov. 30, 1907.

Hanley, Joseph. Born Aug. 12, 1901. Died March 31, 1907. Age 6 y 9 m 18 d. Burial date April 1, 1907.

Harper, William. Died Feb. 1, 1919. Age about 50 yrs. Burial date Feb. 3, 1919.

Harper, Wm. Henry. Died Aug. 16, 1903. Age 1 y 2 m.

Harris, Lucy. Died May 3, 1912. Age 28 y. Burial date May 5, 1912.

Harris, Simon. Born 1849. Died Nov. 5, 1903. Age 54 y 6 m. (Source of birth date: WPA)

Harris, Susan B. Died July 13, 1911. Age about 80 yrs. Burial date July 18, 1911.

Hart, Hellena. Born Jan. 24, 1911. Died April 28, 1912. Age 1 y 3 m 4 d. Burial date April 30, 1912.

Hartwell, Jack. Born Oct. 5, 1875. Died Jan. 11, 1907. Age 32 y 3 m 6 d. Burial date Jan. 15, 1907.

Harvey, Francis. Born Jan. 12, 1905. Died Oct. 6, 1906. Age 9 m. Burial date Oct. 7, 1906.

Hawkins, Laura L. Born Nov. 15, 1850. Died Sept. 28, 1907. Age 57 y 10 m 13 d. Burial date Oct. 1, 1907.

Hawkins,Thos.Vincon. Born Dec.7, 1909. Died Aug. 16, 1911. Age 1 y 8 m 8 d. Burial date Aug. 18, 1911.

Heartwell, Jack. Died July 28, 1910. Age about 68 yrs. Burial date July 31, 1910.

Henderson, J.H. Died Nov. 6, 1916. Age 66 y. Burial date Nov. 9, 1916.

Henderson, Oscar M. Born 1866. Died April 8, 1916. Age 50 y. Burial date April 10, 1916.

Hill, Wallace. Born March 1862. Died Dec. 22, 1908. Age 46 y 9 m. Burial date Dec. 24, 1908.

Hill, Zenobia. Born Sept. 10, 1910. Died Feb. 2, 1911. Age 5 m 8 d. Burial date Feb. 4, 1911.

Hogsette, Charles H. (no information available)

Hogsette, Olaf. Born Aug. 31, 1894. Died June 22, 1914. Age 20 y 9 m 22 d. Burial date June 25, 1914.

Hurst, Strus. Born Sept. 27, 1895. Died Sept. 15, 1912. Age 17 y 3 d. Burial date Sept. 17, 1912.

Hurst, T. Born Jan. 5, 1907. Died Jan. 6, 1908. Age l y 1 d. Burial date Jan. 8, 1908.

Hurst, Zelma M. Born Oct. 5, 1908. Died Nov. 18, 1910. Age 2 y 1 m. Burial date Nov. 20, 1910.

Irvin, Chas. Died March 20, 1914. Age 50 y. Burial date March 23, 1914.

Jackson, Andrew. Died Feb. 13, 1908. Age 63 y. Burial date Feb. 16, 1908.

Jackson, Early F. Born Feb. 22, 1885. Died March 13, 1907. Age 22 y 1 m 7 d. Burial date March 17, 1907.

Jackson, Herbert. Born Dec. 20, 1900. Died March 13, 1918. Age 17 y 2 m 21 d. Burial date March 15, 1918.

Jackson, Janie. Born Aug. 12, 1912. Died Sept. 25, 1913. Age l y l m 5 d. Burial date Sept. 28, 1913.

Jackson, Martin. Born Nov. 2, 1850. Died Oct. 15, 1906. Age 56 y. Burial date Oct. 15, 1906.

Jackson, Mary Jane. Born Jan. 1, 1847. Died Feb. 15, 1909. Age 62 y 1 m 14 d. Burial date Feb. 18, 1909.

James, Rossie B. Born Jan. 29, 1912. Died Jan. 29, 1912. Age 15 hours. Burial date Jan. 30, 1912.

James, Wilson. Born Dec. 1, 1850. Died July 10, 1917. Age 66 y 7 m 9 d. Burial date July 13, 1917.

James, Wilson J.B. Born Sept. 28, 1891. Died Feb. 13, 1917. Age 25 y 4 m 15 d. Burial date Feb. 16, 1917.

Jenkins, Flora J. Born June 10, 1899. Died April 7, 1918. Age 19 y 9 m 28 d. Burial date April 9, 1918.

Jenkins, Mildred Hester. Born March 29, 1918. Died Oct. 7, 1918. Age 6 m 8 d. Burial date Oct. 9, 1918.

Jewett, Alfred (Albert S.) Born Dec. 25, 1833. Died April 28, 1902. Age 64 y 4 m.

Jewett, Ioola. Born Aug. 27, 1911. Died April 20, 1912. Age 7 m 20 d. Burial date April 22, 1912.

Jobes, Elverta. Born May ?, ?. Died Jan. 15, 1908. Age 21 y 9 m. Burial date Jan. 18, 1908.

Johnson, Ada. Born 1857. Died 1919.

Johnson, Albert. Born June 5, ?. Died April 21, 1911. Age 24 y 11 m 13 d. Burial date April 23, 1911.

Johnson, Anna M. Born Feb. 2, 1907. Died June 24, 1907. Age 4 m. Burial date June 25, 1907.

Johnson, Henry. Born Feb. 20, 1886. Died Dec. 20,1907. Age 21 y 11 m. Burial date Dec. 22, 1907.

Johnson, Infant. Born June 11, 1906. Died July 1, 1906. Age 21 d. Burial date July 2, 1906.

Johnson, James.* Born Dec. 14, 1885. Died April 22, 1915.

Johnson, John D. Born April 28, 1866. Died May 26, 1909. Age 43 y 28 d. Burial date May 29, 1909.

Johnson, Lola M. Born March 29, 1906. Died Dec. 14, 1908. Age 2 y 8 m 15 d. Burial date Dec. 19, 1908.

Johnson, Ned.* Died Jan. 23, 1910. Aged 54 y.

Johnson, Ollie M. Born Feb. 21, 1906. Died March 7, 1908. Age 2 y 17 d. Burial date March 9, 1908.

Johnson, Willard J. Born May 16, 1910. Died Aug. 2, 1910. Age 2 m.16 d. Burial date Aug. 3,1910.

Jones, Ann. Born Dec. 24, 1835. Died Oct. 15, 1906. Age 70 y 9 m 20 d. Burial date Oct. 17, 1906

Jones, Floyd. Born June 8, 1884. Died Sept. 2, 1916. Age 52 y 2 m 25 d. Burial date Sept. 4, 1916

Jones, Franklin Taylor. Died Nov. 23, 1922. Age 3 m 24 d. Burial date Nov. 29, 1922.

Jones, Hattie. Born July 4, 1889. Died June 25, 1909. Age 20 y 11 m 21 d. Burial date June 27, 1909

Jones, Howard Richard. Born April 18, 1912. Died April 20, 1912. Age 2 d. Burial date April 23, 1912.

Jones, Lilly Mrs. Born Nov. 24, 1883. Died June 3, 1913. Age 30 y 7 m 21 d. Burial date June 5, 1913.

Jones, Rudolph. Born July 4, 1913. Died Aug. 27, 1913. Age 1 m 23 d. Burial date Aug. 28, 1913.

Jones, Shimetta. Born May 2, 1910. Died Sept. 30, 1910. Age 5 m. Burial date Oct. 2, 1910.

Jones, Walter. Born April 15, 1906. Died Jan. 10, 1907. Age 7 m. Burial date Jan. 12, 1907.

Kenedy, Mary Ida. Died Oct. 16, 1903. Age 23 y.

King, Ethel. Died Oct. 8, 1911. Age about 21 yrs. Burial date Oct. 10, 1911.

Lawson, Lina. Born 1880. Died Dec. 26, 1913. Age 33 y 3 m. Burial date Dec. 28, 1913.

Lee, Helen. Born Dec. 16, 1908. Died April 2, 1909. Age 4 m 6 d. Burial date April 23, 1909.

Lee, John W. Born Dec. 21, 1910. Died Dec. 24, 1910. Age 3 d. Burial date Dec. 24, 1910.

Lee, Melvina Alberta. Born Dec. 9, 1883. Died Dec. 28, 1914. Age 31 y 19 d. Burial date Dec. 29, 1914.

Lee, Sadia G. Born April 28, 1907. Died Jan. 15, 1908. Age 8 m 8 d. Burial date Jan. 17, 1908.

Lee, W.W. Born Dec. 7, ?. Died Oct. 16, 1913. Age 42 y 10 m 9 d. Burial date Oct. 19, 1913.

Lewis, Lex H. Born Jan. 9, 1907. Died Jan. 16, 1907. Age 1 week. Burial date Jan. 17, 1907.

Lippard, Richard. Died April 11, 1902. Age 2 y 11 m.

Logan, Mazura. Born May 6, 1876. Died May 8, 1915. Age 48 y 2 d. Burial date May 1915.

Louis, Lee Drew. Born Jan. 6, 1906. Died Aug. 10, 1906. Age 7 m 5 d. Burial date Aug. 11, 1906.

Lynch, Infant. Born Aug. 5, 1907. Died Aug. 5, 1907. Burial date Aug. 5, 1907.

Lynch, Richard. Born July 30, 1906. Died Nov. 15, 1906. Age 3 m 15 d. Burial date Nov. 15, 1906.

Lyons, C.J. Died March 19, 1914. Age about 45y. Burial date March 22, 1914.

Marshall, Hill. Born Aug. 1 5, 1854. Died March 6, 1915. Age 60 y 6 m 20 d. Burial date March 7, 1915.

Mascara, Antonie. Born Oct. 2, 1894. Died Nov. 17, 1918. Age 24 y 1 m 15 d. Burial date Nov. 20, 1918.

Mason, Beatrice. Born Aug. 1, 1907. Died Dec. 25, 1907. Age 5 m 24 d. Burial date Dec. 26, 1907.

Mason, John W. Died April 10, 1907. Age 40 y. Burial date April 12, 1907.

Massey, Annie J. Born April 2, 1910. Died Sept. 29, 1910. Age 5 m 28 d. Burial date Sept. 30, 1910.

Massey, Horace. Born Aug. 5, 1861. Died July 19, 1906. Age 41 y 11 m 14 d. Burial date July 22, 1906.

Mathew, William.* Born 1869. Died July 15, 1910.

Mathews, Stewart. Born March 10, 1854. Died March 22, 1914. Age 60 y. Burial date March 25, 1914.

Mauson, Mary. Died Aug. 31, 1902. Age 58 y 3 m 24 d.

McDonald, Robert. Born Feb. 1, 1909. Died Sept. 5, 1910. Age 1 y. Burial date Sept. 6, 1910.

McDonel, Eva. Born July 3, 1906. Died April 13, 1907. Age 1 y 8 m 10 d. Burial date April 14, 1907.

McKemson, Maxsine. Born March 22, 1917. Died March 22, 1917. Stillborn. Burial date March 22, 1917.

McKinney, Bernice. Born Aug. 7, 1911. Died June 24, 1918. Age 6 y 10 m 17 d. Burial date June 26, 1918.

McKinney, James (Jay). Born Dec. 24, 1875. Died Sept. 19, 1923. Age about 50 yrs. Burial date Sept. 21, 1923.

McKinnie, Effie Mrs. Born May 5, 1884. Died April 7, 1913. Age 29 y 11 m 28 d. Burial date April 9, 1913.

Mease, Leo Hobart. Born Feb. 13, 1896. Died Feb. 23, 1911. Age 16 y 10 d. Burial date Feb. 25, 1911.

Miachal, Ed Lee.* Born May 20, 1910. Died Nov. 16, 1910.

Michael, Cortelia. Born June 30, 1873. Died Oct. 19, 1913. Age 40 y 3 m 20 d. Burial date Oct. 22, 1913.

Michael, Frank.* Born June 26, 1912. Died Oct. 23, 1912.

Michael, Mary E.* Died Sept. 22, 1907. Aged 70 y.

Mickens, Mary Mrs. Died Aug. 15, 1912. Age about 60 yrs. Burial date Aug. 18,1912.

Miller, Brisco. Died Dec. 20, 1912. Age about 61 yrs. Burial date Dec. 23, 1912.

Miller, Fanny May. Born March 4, 1900. Died June 18, 1914. Age 14 y 3 m 12 d. Burial date June 18, 1914.

Miller, George W. Born Sept. 2, 1841. Died Sept. 10, 1917. Age 76 y 8 d. Burial date Sept. 12, 1917.

Miller, Infant. Born Nov. 8, 1906. Died Nov. 8, 1906. Burial date Nov. 9, 1906.

Miller, Margaret Mrs. Born Oct. 20, 1881. Died Jan. 11, 1911. Age 29 y 3 m 11 d. Burial date Jan. 15, 1911.

Miller, Sallie. Died Aug. 15, 1923. Age about 58 yrs. Burial date Aug. 17, 1923.

Milton, Infant. Born Aug. 12, 1907. Died Sept. 13, 1907. Age 1 m 1 d. Burial date Sept. 14, 1907.

Minor, George Thomas. Died April 25, 1911. Age 57 y. Burial date April 30, 1911.

Moman, James. Died June 19, 1909. Age about 43 yrs. Burial date June 20, 1909.

Moppin, Grace. Born April 24, 1855. Died Oct. 28, 1908. Age 53 y 6 m 4 d. Burial date Nov. 1, 1908.

Morgan, Infant. Born Dec. 29, 1912. Died Dec. 29, 1912. Stilllborn. Burial date Dec. 30, 1912.

Morgan, Infant. Born Oct. 12, 1914. Died Oct. 12, 1914. Age 4 hours. Burial date Oct. 14, 1914.

Morgan, Jame P. Born July 8, 1911. Died June 18, 1913. Age 2 y 11 m 20 d. Burial date June 19, 1913.

Morrison, Melva. Born March 2, 1911. Died May 18, 1912. Age l y 1 m 1 6 d. Burial date May 20, 1912.

Muray, Tommy.* Born Feb. 10, 1908. Died Dec. 7, 1908

Murray, Vernon. Born Oct. 19, 1907. Died Sept. 23, 1908. Age 11 m 4 d. Burial date Sept. 25, 1908.

Nichols, Rossie. Born March 16, 1901. Died April 3, 1912. Age 11 y 0 m 17 d. Burial date April 5, 1912.

Norse, Jacob. Born 1878. Died Dec. 14, 1915. Age 37 y. Burial date Dec. 16, 1915.

Novak, Mary. Born Sept. 3, 1911. Died Sept. 14, 1911. Age 11 d. Burial date Sept. 15, 1911.

Oksji, Infant. Died Sept. 25, 1913. Stillborn. Burial date Sept. 26, 1913.

Oksji, Mary. Born Sept. 29, 1912. Died Sept. 29, 1912. Stillborn. Burial date Sept. 30, 1912.

Oliphant, Caroline. Died March 4, 1914. Age 61 y. Burial date March 6, 1914.

Onsley, Lillian. Born June 25, 1893. Died June 22, 1918. Age 24 y11 m 28 d. Burial date June 24, 1918.

Ousley, Williebelie. Born June 8, 1918. Died Dec. 7, 1918. Age 5 m 29 d. Burial date Dec. 9, 1918.

Parker, Dorothy. Born Sept. 28, 1908. Died Dec. 16, 1910. Age 2 y 3 m. Burial date Dec. 17, 1910.

Parker, Hattie. Born Sept. 26 1883. Died March 11, 1908. Age 25 y 5 m 15 d. Burial date March 12, 1908.

Parker, Hattie. Born March 1, 1908. Died March 7, 1908. Burial date March 9, 1908.

Parker, Henry Chas. Born Oct. 9, 1910. Died March 5, 1911. Age 4 m 27 d. Burial date March 6, 1911.

Parker, Wiley. Born Nov. 15, 1858. Died Oct. 10, 1915. Age 56 y 10 m 25 d. Burial date Oct. 13, 1915.

Parkey, Infant. Born Feb. 17, 1914. Died Feb. 20, 1914. Age 4 d. Burial date Feb. 21, 1914.

Parkey, Walter. Born Aug. 22, 1907. Died May 28, 1907. Burial date May 29, 1907.

Patterson, George. Born 1853. Died May 8, 1916. Age 63 y. Burial date May 10, 1916.

Patterson, William G. Born June 25, 1894. Died. Nov. 10, 1912. Age 18 y 4 m 15 d. Burial date Nov. 12, 1912.

Peaso, Samuel H. Born Dec. 10, 1869. Died July 12, 1915. Age 45 y 7 m 2 d. Burial date July 15, 1915.

Perkins, Martha. Born March 10, 1853. Died May 17, 1909. Wife of W. Anderson Perkins.

Perkins, W. Anderson. Born July 5, 1853. May 3, 1909. Civil War Veteran. (Source: WPA)

Peterson, Herbert.* Born Aug. 21, 1888. Died Feb. 3, 1913.

Poe, Add. Born Feb. 20, 1879. Died May 3, 1914. Age 35 y 2 m 2 d. Burial date May 5, 1914.

Pollock, Geo. Dewey. Born Dec. 5, 1898. Died May 14, 1916. Age 17 y 5 m 9 d. Burial date May 16, 1916.

Pondexter, Rease. Died April 28, 1911. Age about 79 yrs. Burial date April 30, 1911.

Prentice, Mrs. Samuel.* Born Aug. 1858. Died Oct. 14, 1907.

Price, Annie Bell. Born June 19, 1862. Died July 30, 1914. Age 52 y 1 m 21 d. Burial date Aug. 1, 1914.

Pugh, Infant. Born May 21, 1914. Died May 21, 1914. Stillborn. Burial date May 22, 1914.

Pugh, Mary Frances. Born March 16, 1917. Died March 16, 1917. Stillborn. Burial date March 17, 1917.

Quails, Lefern. Born Nov. 6, 1911. Died Dec. 6, 1911. Age 1 m. Burial date Dec. 7, 1911.

Railey, John R. (No information.)

Randolph, John Wm. Died April 14, 1911. Age 17 y. 1 d. Burial date April 16, 1911.

Ray, Florence. Born Feb. 24, 1906. Died July 30, 1912. Age 6 y 5 m 4 d. Burial date Aug. 1, 1912.

Reasby, Clifton. Born April 20, 1903. Died May 21, 1910.

Reasby, Lucy Mrs. Born 1876. Died April 7, 1910.

Reasby, Mary. Born March 1 3, 1914. Died Aug. 1 3, 1914. Age 5 m. Burial date Aug. 15, 1914.

Reasby, Ralph. Born April 20, 1907. Died April 27, 1907.

Reasby, Rosa M. Born April 6, 1910. Died April 6, 1910.

Reaves, Elex Mr. Died Aug. 6, 1910. Age 55 y. Burial date Aug. 10, 1910.

Reaves, Wm. H. Died May 6, 1907. Age 63 y. Burial date May 8, 1907.

Reed, Leona. Born July 4, 1882. Died May 13, 1907. Age 25 y 10 m 9 d. Burial date May 13, 1907.

Reeves, Chas. Edward. Born Oct. 16, 1898. Died Nov. 21, 1916. Age 18 y 1 m 5 d. Burial date Nov. 23, 1916.

Reeves, Ella. Died Oct. 1, 1916. Age 37 y. Burial date Oct. 2, 1916.

Reeves, Peter. Born 1850. Died Sept. 28, 1917. Age 67 y. Burial date Oct. 2, 1917.

Rhoads, Eldora Taylor. Born April 25, 1885. Died Oct. 21, 1913. Age 29 y 5 m 11 d. Burial date Oct. 25, 1913.

Rhoads, James Bill. Born June 5, 1891. Died May 1, 1911. Age 19 y 10 m 16 d. Burial date May 4, 1911.

Rhodes, Ernest. Born March 4, 1896. Died Feb. 16, 1907. Age 11 y. Burial date Feb. 17, 1907.

Rhodes, Hubert Lincoln. Died May 26, 1903. Age 6 y.

Rhodes, Isac LeRoy. Born Jan. 30, 1912. Died Sept. 4, 1912. Age 7 m 4 d. Burial date Sept. 5, 1912.

Richey, Clifford Odell. Born Nov. 13, 1910. Died Feb. 22, 1911. Age 3 m 9 d. Burial date Feb. 23, 1911.

Riggs, Elizabeth L. Died March 20, 1905.

Roberts, Clem. Died Jan. 18, 1908. Age 37. Burial date Jan. 19, 1908.

Roberts, Jim. Born July 4, 1853. Died Nov. 5, 1907. Age 54 4 1 d. Burial date Nov. 7, 1907.

Roberts, Lenard. Died Sept. 20, 1916. Age 66 y. Burial date Oct. 4, 1916.

Robinson, Infant. Born April 16, 1907. Died April 16, 1907. Stillborn. Burial date April 17, 1907.

Robinson, Martha. Born April 1894. Died Dec. 6, 1906. Age 12 y 9 m. Burial date Dec. 9, 1906.

Robinson, Wm. A. Born Aug. 18, 1906. Died Aug. 25, 1906. Age 7 d. Burial date Aug. 26, 1906.

Rollette, Selestine M. Born July 25, 1912. Died May 30, 1913. Age 10 m 6 d. Burial date June 1, 1913.

Buxton Cemetery, 2007. Stones in the Buxton cemetery represent 41 individuals, but more than 400 persons are known to have been buried there. (Michael W. Lemberger)

Ross, Coy Jackson.* Born Feb. 3, 1806. Died Oct. 29, 1909

Rowlette, G. Mrs. Born Feb. 2, 1880. Died March 13, 1913. Age 33 y 1 m 12 d. Burial date March 16, 1913.

Sandridge, Henry. Born 1860. Died May 14, 1916. Age 56 y. Burial date May 17, 1916.

Scales, Frank. Born Jan. 2, 1897. Died Sept. 5, 1918. Age 21 y 8 m 3 d. Burial date Sept. 9, 1918.

Scales, Raman. Born July 18, 1904. Died Jan. 20, 1907. Age 2 y 6 m. Burial date Jan. 22, 1907.

Seales, Robert. Died Sept. 22, 1907. Age 42 y. Burial date Sept. 24, 1907.

Sebban, John Jr.* Born Oct. 10, 1916. Died Oct. 12, 1916

Sedlock, Infant. Born Dec. 6, 1912. Died Dec. 6, 1912. Stillborn. Burial date Dec. 6, 1912.

Sellers, Hattie. Born 1862. Died Aug. 15, 1914. Age 52 y 4 m. Burial date Aug. 17, 1914.

Shades, James. Born Jan. 2, 1868. Died June 4, 1911. Age 43 y 6 m 2 d. Burial date June 6, 1911.

Sharp, Harry. Born May 23, 1917. Died Feb. 4, 1918. Age 8 m 11 d. Burial date Feb. 5, 1918.

Shelton, Orvall S. Born June 26, 1906. Died July 22, 1906. Age 27 d. Burial date July 24, 1906.

Shepherd, Martha Reasby. Died June 21, 1918. Burial date June 23, 1918.

Shepherd, Willie C. Born May 8, 1906. Died Jan. 10, 1907. Age 8 m. Burial date Jan. 12, 1907

Simms, D.S. Died Feb. 8, 1918. Age about 45 yrs. Burial date Feb. 10, 1918.

Skipworth, William I. Born Aug. 24, 1884. Died Aug. 25, 1912. Age 28 y. Burial date Aug. 28, 1912.

Slaughter, King. Born March 10, 1861. Died May 14, 1915. Age 54 y 2 m 4 d. Burial date May 17, 1915.

Smith, Alonda. Born July 27, 1906. Died Jan. 25, 1907. Age 6 m 2 d. Burial date Jan. 27, 1907.

Smith, Daniel G.* Born July 16, 1890. Died Jan. 13, 1910. (Mahaska County Death Records list birth date as Feb. 13, 1890; Born Iowa.) Source: WPA.

Smith, Infant. Born July 14, 1907. Died Aug. 19, 1907. Age 1 m 5 d. Burial date Aug. 20, 1907.

Smith, Infant. Born Jan. 1910. Died April 2, 1911. Burial date April 3, 1911.

Smith, Jaml Edd.* Born July 16, 1867. Died March 8, 1918.

Smith, John H. Born June 5, 1850. Died Aug. 21, 1906. Age 56 y 2 m 21 d. Burial date Aug. 24, 1906.

Smith, Oscar.* Born Sept. 15, 1889. Died Jan. 21, 1913.

Smith, Sam. Died April 20, 1909. Age about 95 yrs. Burial date April 24, 1909.

Smith, W.H. Died 1910.

Snell, William. Died Feb. 15, 1912. Age about 70 yrs. Burial date Feb. 17, 1912.

Soles, Mary Annie. Born May 15, 1916. Died Sept. 1, 1917. Age 1 y 3 m 16 d. Burial date Sept. 1, 1917.

Sorrell, Infant. Born Dec. 5, 1906. Died Dec. 5, 1906. Burial date Dec. 6, 1906.

Southall, Wm. Died Feb. 13, 1907. Age 46 y. Burial date Feb. 14, 1907.

Southerland, Wm. M. Born June 2, 1868. Died May 11, 1915. Age 46 y 11 m 9 d. Burial date May 13, 1915.

Stewart, Martha Perkins. Born March 10, 1883. Died May 17, 1900. (Death certificate lists birth year as 1882 and death date as May 17, 1909.)

Stokes, George W. Born Nov. 1875. Died Dec. 6, 1915. Age 40 y 1 m. Burial date Dec. 8, 1915.

Sykes, Maud. Born May 22, 1893. Died March 12, 1918. Age 24 y 11 m 20 d. Burial date March 15, 1918.

Tanks, James. Died Nov. 28, 1906. Age 60 y. Burial date Nov. 30, 1906.

Taylor, Infant. Born May 19, 1907 Died May 19, 1907. Age 12 hours. Burial date May 20, 1907.

Taylor, Mathew. Died Nov. 8, 1910. Age about 33 yrs. Burial date Nov. 13, 1910.

Taylor, Shelby M. Born Dec. 8, 1886. Died Sept. 7, 1906. Age 10 y 8 m. Burial date Sept. 9, 1906.

Taylor, Sloan. Born June 7, 1894. Died Jan. 8, 1917. Age 22 y 7 m. Burial date Jan. 10, 1917.

Thomas, Bessie. Died April 28, 1908. Age 47 y. Burial date May 1, 1908.

Thomas, Calvin. Born Jan. 10, 1919. Died Jan. 10, 1919. Age 12 hours. Burial date Jan. 11, 1919.

Thomas, Darlene. Born Dec. 10, 1907. Died Aug. 19, 1908. Age 8 m 9 d. Burial date Aug. 20, 1908.

Thomas, Henrietta. Born Dec. 12, 1863. Died April 12, 1916. Age 52 y 4 m. Burial date April 14, 1916.

Thomas, James. Died Sept. 14, 1913. Burial date Sept. 15, 1913.

Thompson, Carry. Born March 1870. Died Aug. 1, 1906. Age 36 y. Burial date Aug. 3, 1906.

Toliver, John Sr. Born March 1850. Died Oct. 26, 1907. Age 57 y 7 m. Burial date Oct. 27, 1907.

Tolliver, J. W.* Born Dec. 13, 1871. Died March 19, 1908.

Tolson, Francis.* Born Nov. 19, 1918. Died April 30, 1919.

Tolson, Fred. Born July 24, 1889. Died Dec. 13, 1915. Age 26 y 4 m 19 d. Burial date Dec. 15, 1915.

Tolson, Roy McK. Born March 4, ?. Died Dec. 9, 1908. Age 11 y 9 m.

Toran, Lorenzo Little. Born Aug. 20, 1910. Died Feb. 27, 1912. Age 2 y 6 m 7 d. Burial date March 1, 1912.

Rock marking grave. (Michael W. Lemberger)

Troutner, Charles. Died Oct. 1918.

Turner, Child. Died July 28, 1910. Age 6 m. Burial date July 30, 1910.

Turner, Eugene. Born May 11, 1914. Died Oct. 7, 1914. Age 29 y 4 m 26 d. Burial date Oct. 10, 1914.

Turner, Infant. Born Aug. 6, 1915. Died Aug. 6, 1915. Stillborn. Burial date Aug. 7, 1915.

Turner, Sallie. Born 1850. Died Oct. 24, 1909. Age 59 y 2 m. (WPA records give death date as Oct 26, 1909.)

Vipond, Infant. Born Sept. 27, 1917. Died Sept. 27, 1917. Stillborn. Burial date Sept. 27, 1917.

Walker, Charles.* Born 1868. Died July 18, 1913.

Walker, George Washington. Born Feb. 15, 1867. Died June 16, 1903. Age 37 y 4 m 1 d.

Walker, John. Died May 25, 1923. Age 70 y.

Walker, Lewis W. Born Jan. 8, 1906. Died Nov.16, 1907. Age 1 y 10 m 11 d. Burial date Nov.19, 1907.

Walker, Pauline. Born Feb. 28, 1874. Died March 31, 1915. Age 41 y 1 m 3 d. Burial date April 3, 1915.

Ward, Bell. Died Oct. 2, 1916. Age 49 y. Burial date Oct. 5, 1916.

Ward, Robert. Born Feb. 10, 1865. Died April 25, 1914. Age 49 y 2 m 15 d. Burial date April 27, 1914.

Washington, William. Born 1893. Died 1926.

Watkins, B. Born June 15, 1885. Died Dec. 18, 1908. Age 23 y 6 m 18 d. Burial date Dec. 21, 1908.

Watkins, Samie. Born July 14, 1881. Died Sept. 2, 1907. Age 26 y 1 m 17 d. Burial date Sept. 5, 1907.

Watkins, Thomas. Born April 19, 1872. Died May 5, 1914. Age 42 y 17 d. Burial date May 7, 1914.

Watkins, W.J. Born Dec. 19, 1906. Died Sept. 28, 1907. Age 8 m 9 d. Burial date Sept. 29, 1907.

Watson, Susie E. Born Oct. 1, 1898. Died April 5, 1914. Age 16 y 6 m 4 d. Burial date April 7, 1914.

Webster, Robert. Born 1856. Died July 29, 1908. Age 52 y. Burial date Aug. 2, 1908.

Welch, Ellen. Born Feb. 14, 1837. Died Dec. 28, 1916. Age 79 y 10 m 14 d.

Wesley, James Edman.* Born Feb. 2, 1861. Died Feb. 22, 1913.

Wesley, Lionel. Died April 18, 1902. Age 1 y 11 m.

Wesley, Sarah. Born Feb. 8, 1866. Died Nov. 20, 1908. Age 42 y 9 m 12 d. Burial date Nov. 22, 1908.

West, Frank Jr. Died April 9, 1923. Age 4 m 2 d. Burial date April 11, 1923

West. Lee Andrew. Born Oct. 20, 1877. Died May 25, 1916. Age 38 y 7 m 5 d. Burial date May 28, 1916.

Weston, John. Born Dec. 25, 1829. Died Nov. 11, 1913. Age 83 y 1 m 17 d. Burial date Nov. 13, 1913.

Wheels, Dora. Born November, ?. Died Sept. 15, 1906. Age 21 y. Burial date Sept. 17, 1906

White, Bula. Born May 14, 1911. Died Aug. 14, 1911. Age 3 m. Burial date Aug. 15, 1911.

White, Dunn. Died July 4, 1912. Age 65 y. Burial date July 6, 1912.

Williams, Beatrice. Born Jan. 1885. Died Oct. 5, 1906. Age 19 y. Burial date Oct. 6, 1906.

Williams, Celia. Born Jan. 15, 1876. Died July 4, 1907. Age 31 y 7 m 11 d. Burial date July 6, 1907.

Williams, Charlie. Born March 1, 1852. Died March 5, 1907. Age 55 y 5 d. Burial date March 7, 1907.

Williams, Earl.* Born March 31, 1911. Died April 19, 1911

Williams, Emma. Born Sept. 25, 1872. Died Jan. 12, 1907. Age 35 y. Burial date Jan. 14, 1907.

Williams, Infant. Born Sept. 29, 1906. Died Sept. 29, 1906. Burial date Sept. 29, 1906.

Williams, John M. Died April 22, 1909. Age about 55 yrs. Burial date April 1909.

Williams, John W. Born March 7, 1882. Died March 18, 1914. Age about 27 y. Burial date March 21, 1914.

Williams, Sidney. Died July 28, 1914. Age 61 y. Burial date July 30, 1914.

Willis, George. Born Oct. 20, 1875. Died Oct. 28, 1907. Age 32 y 8 d. Burial date Nov. 1, 1907.

Willis, George A. Born Aug. 18, 1889. Died March 5, 1908. Age 19 y 5m 13 d. Burial date March 8, 1908.

Wilson, Bettie. Died Jan. 26, 1912. Age 66 y.

Wilson, Cornelius W. Born March 19, 1904. Died Jan. 7, 1907. Age 2 y 10 m. Burial date Jan. 9, 1907.

Wilson, Jerry. Born 1841 Died March 24, 1907. Age 66 y. Burial date March 25, 1907.

Wilson, Samuel. Born Aug. 8, 1849. Died Feb. 18, 1911. Age 62 y 7 m 10 d. Burial date Feb. 21, 1911.

Winston, Lucey. Born June 10, 1827. Died May 6, 1915. Age 87 y 10 m 26 d. Burial date May 9, 1915.

Winston, Robert. Born Oct. 15, ?. Died April 18, 1907. Age 44 y 5 m 5 d. Burial date April 21, 1907.

Wood, Alpha L.O. Born Aug. 22, 1905. Died April 5, 1907. Age 1 y 7 m 14 d. Burial date April 7, 1907.

Wood, Mary W. Born Feb. 6, 1835. Died Aug. 23, 1906. Age 71 y 7 m 19 d. Burial date Aug. 25, 1906.

Woodfolk, Vera Ann. Born May 30, 1889. Died Sept. 27, 1907. Age 18 y 3 m 27 d. Burial date Sept. 29, 1907.

Woodford, George. Born Feb. 3, 1889. Died May 8, 1911. Age 22 y 4 m 5 d. Burial date May 11, 1911.

Woodfork, Robert. Died June 25, 1908. Age 40 y. Burial date June 29, 1908.

Woodley, Leatha. Born July 3, 1895. Died May 6, 1919. Age 23 y 10 m 3 d.

Woods, Mary. Born Dec. 8, 1906. Died Feb. 18, 1912. Age 5 y 1 m 10 d. Burial date Feb. 21, 1912.

Young, Augusta. Born Aug. 6, 1875. Died Jan. 7, 1917. Age 41 y 5 m 1 d. Burial date Jan. 9, 1917.

Young, Edward C. Born Jan. 27, 1916. Died Jan. 28, 1917. Age 1 y 1 d. Burial date Jan. 30, 1917.

Young, Infant. Born Aug. 8, 1913. Died Aug. 9, 1913. Age 1 d. Burial date Aug. 10, 1913.

Sources:

* – Mahaska County, Iowa, death record indexes. No ages or burial dates are listed in these indexes.

1935 Pension Records for Monroe County, Iowa
(African-American residents)

Bluff Creek Township:

Gaines, Reuben, Rt. 1 Albia, Born: Nov. 26, 1888 in Nebraska, Father: Rueben Gaines, Mother: Elizabeth Kenney
Gaines, Anna, Rt. 1 Albia, Born: June 18, 1898 in Tennessee, Father: Aaron Northcutt, Mother: Anna Wenton
Humbles, Frank, Rt. 2 Lovilia, Born: Dec. 15, 1867 in Virginia, Father: Mack Humbles, Mother: Frances Ross
Harris, Henry, Rt. 2 Lovilia, Born: April 11, 1857 in Virginia, Father: Robert Harris, Mother: Martha Harris
Jenkins, John B., Rt. 2 Lovilia, Born: Sept. 2, 1876 in Missouri, Father: Benjamin Jenkins, Mother: Hester Lyrens
Jenkins, Irene, Rt. 2 Lovilia, Born: March 25, 1884 in Oklahoma, Father: Unnamed McCoy, Mother: Not Given
Jenkins, Hester, Rt. 2 Lovilia, Born: Feb. 20, 1841 in Missouri, Father: Unnamed Lyrens, Mother: Matilda Johnson
Johnson, Duncan, County Farm, Born: Dec. 25, 1853 in Mississippi, Father: Thomas Johnson, Mother: Not Given
Mosby, Fred, County Farm, Born: May 9, 1865 in West Virginia, Parents Names Not Given
Mosby, Julia, County Farm, Born: 1854 in Virginia, Parents Names Not Given
Moore, Aubra, Rt. 2 Lovilia, Born: Aug. 20, 1883 in Virginia, Father: Peter Moore, Mother: Sue Chetum
Madison, Archie, Rt. 2 Lovilia, Born: March 1886 in Virginia, Father: Archie Madison, Mother: Sarah Grievous
Madison, Minnie, Rt. 2 Lovilia, Born: March 16, 1885 in Virginia, Father: John Lesley, Mother: Lizzie Jackson
Vaughn, Sarah, Rt. 2, Lovilia, Born: March 1, 1860 in Virginia, Father: Foutain Grevies, Mother; Jane Bias
Wright, Hiram, Rt. 2, Lovilia, Born: Nov. 30, 1863 in Virginia, Father: Hiram Wright, Mother: Judea Wright
Wright, Jennie, Rt. 2 Lovilia, Born: Dec. 25, 1866 in Virginia, Father: Unnamed Jones, Mother: Sallie E. Desper
Washington, James H., Rt. 2 Lovilia, Born: March 11, 1867 in Virginia, Father: Bush Rod Washington, Mother: Harriet Childs

Guilford Township:

Boles, Mary Catharine, No Residence, Born: June 15, 1866 in Winchester, Virginia, Father: Richard Thompson, Mother: Martha Washington
Boles, Stephen, Hiteman, Born: Sept. 1, 1975 in Fluvatina, Virginia, Father: George W. Boles, Mother: Betty Ware
Cathron, Charles William, Hiteman, Born: March 1, 1870 in Courtland, Alabama, Father: Charles Cathron, Mother: Emily Moe
Lewis, John Randolph, Hiteman, Born; Aug. 24, 1854 in Richmond, Virginia, Father: Griffith R. Lewis, Mother: Pru Ann Lewis
Lewis, Nannie, Hiteman, Born: Dec. 25, 1878 in Fluvanna Co., Virginia, Father: George W. Boles, Mother: Betty Ware
Randolph, Henry Thomas, Hiteman, Born: Dec. 27, 1848 in Virginia, Father: Jesse Randolph, Mother: Vinia Good
Randolph, Lucy Ann, Hiteman, Born: May 18, 1863 in Virginia, Father: George Boles, Mother: Betty Ware

Troy Township:

Burns, Verga, Albia, Born: Aug. 1, 1870 in Virginia, Father: Unnamed Nelson, Mother: Unnamed Johnston
Burns, Walter, Albia, Born: March 5, 1866 in North Carolina, Father: John Burns, Mother: Unnamed Freman

Troy Township, Town of Albia: (No Parents are Listed in this Secton)

Brewer, Milo, 506 B. Ave. East, Born: Nov. 30, 1899 in Monroe Co., Iowa, Occupation: Preacher
Brewer, Madlyn, 506 B. Ave. East, Born: July 14, 1909 in Des Moines, Iowa, Wife of Milo

Above and right: A panoramic view of the crowd at a Buxton reunion held in September, 1938.

Dudley, Lewis, 721 C. Ave. East, Born: Jan. 24, 1898 in Missouri, Occupation: Miner
Edmunds, Henry, 424 North B. St., Born: Dec. 1, 1854 in Missouri, Occupation: Miner
Edmunds, Cora, 424 North B. St., Born: Jan. 16, 1888 in Missouri, Wife of Henry
Edmunds, Joe, 704 C. Ave. West, Born: June 18, 1892 in Hocking, Iowa, Occupation: Miner
Edmunds, Mabel, 704 C. Ave. West, Born: Feb. 13, 1895 in Missouri, Wife of Joe
Guy, Alfred, 9 North F. St., Born: July 14, 1890 in Kirksville, Missouri, Occupation: Miner
Guy, Annabelle, 9 North F. St., Born: Dec. 15, 1897 in West Virginia, Wife of Alfred
Grayson, Bennie, 310 7th Ave. West, Born: July 8, 1911 in Hocking, Iowa, Occupation: Janitor
Grayson, LaVinia, 310 7th Ave. West, Born: June 15, 1913 in Hiteman, Iowa, Wife of Bennie
Grayson, Roy, 310 7th Ave. West, Born: Sept. 10, 1882 in Hiteman, Iowa, Occupation: Engineer
Grayson, Bessie, 310 7th Ave. West, Born: Feb. 1, 1888 in Albia, Iowa, Wife of Roy
Gordon, William, North 3rd, Born: Sept. 10, 1870 in West Virginia, Occupation: Laborer
Gordon, Maggie, North 3rd, Born: May 16, 1871 in West Virginia, Wife of William
Hull, George, 611 C. Ave. West, Born: July 13, 1868 in Missouri, Occupation: Laborer
Richards, William, 604 C. Ave. West, Born: June 18, 1865 in Kentucky, Occupation: Miner
Richards, Amanda, 604 C. Ave. West, Born: Jan. 8, 1868 in Florida, Wife of William
Thomas, John, 516 2nd Ave. East, Born: Aug. 22, 1882 in Albia, Iowa, Occupation: Trucker
Thomas, Alice, 516 2nd Ave. East, Born: April 4, 1897 in Wisconsin, Wife of John
Thomas, Pearl, 303 North D., Born: June 10, 1885 in Albia, Iowa, Occupation: Laborer
Thomas, Hazel, 303 North D., Born: Sept. 19, 1904 in Hocking, Iowa, Wife of Pearl

(Lemberger Collection.)

Thomas, Brit, 305 North 5th, Born: Jan. 10, 1880 in Albia, Iowa, Occupation: Laborer
Thomas, Joebell, 305 North 5th, Born: Sept. 16, 1885 in Albia, Iowa, Wife of Brit
Thomas, Edith, 305 North 5th, Born: April 1, 1911 in Albia, Iowa, Occupation: Housework
Williams, T.B., 315 North B., Born: Jan. 22, 1866 in Missouri, Occupation: Laborer
Williams, Mary, 315 North B., Born: Nov. 10, 1890 in Missouri, Wife of T.B.

Union Township:
Buford, John, Rexfield, Born: Oct. 17, 1877 in Virginia, Father: Joshua Buford, Mother: Mary Jane Unnamed
Brooks, Sally, Rexfield, Born: Sept. 21, 1881 in North Carolina, Father: Robert Horrell, Mother: Katherine King
Brooks, Mary Tesser, Rexfield, Born: July 17, 1910 in Buxton, Iowa, Father: William Washington, Mother: Mary Striddling
Brooks, William, Rexfield, Born: Feb. 22, 1877 in Virginia, Father: Jack Brooks, Mother: Not Given
Brooks, George, Rexfield, Born: July 10, 1881 in Virginia, Father: Not Given, Mother: China Brooks
Cox, James Edward, Rexfield, Born: Feb. 9, 1902 in Buxton, Iowa, Father: James Cox, Mother: Pauline Moore
Cox, Luvincie Lillian, Rexfield, Born: Dec. 23, 1905 in Missouri, Father: General Rumley, Mother: Pearl Boyd
Dibbrell, Anna, Rexfield, Born: May 1, 1888 in West Virginia, Father: Peter Moore, Mother: Susie Chithem
Dial, Emma, Rexfield, Born: Dec. 8, 1878 in Missouri, Father: Harrison Fields, Mother: Sarah Harnes
Davis, Rose Ella, Rexfield, Born: Nov. 28, 1877 in Alabama, Father: William Davis, Mother: Maria Davis
Fulton, Issac Nonimus, Rexfield, Born: Nov. 6, 1865 in North Carolina, Parents Not Given
Henderson, Bert, Rexfield, Born: 1875 in Huntsville, Missouri, Father: Hayes Henderson, Mother: Elsie Graves

Henderson, Amanda, Rexfield, Born: May 14, 1879 in Huntsville, Missouri, Father: Kyle Graves, Mother: Caroline Tooley
Jeter, Harry, Rexfield, Born: June 1, 1885 in Centerville, Iowa, Father: Philip Jeter, Mother: Not Given
Johnson, Jessie Maud, Rexfield, Born: July 6, 1894 in West Virginia, Father: Nelson Robinson, Mother: Mary Cooper
Johnson, Frank, Rexfield, Born: April 1, 1864 in Renville, Ohio, Father: Jack Johnson, Mother: None Given
Johnson, Mattie, Rexfield, Born: June 2, 1879 in Madison Co., Kentucky, Father: Turner Reed, Mother: Sarah Fish
Johnson, William, Rexfield, Born: Feb. 20, 1880 in Ohio, Father: Jack Johnson, Mother: Not Given
Johnson, Anna, Rexfield, Born: July 4, 1883 in Munchakinock, Iowa, Father: Moses Gaines, Mother: Maggie Bell
Jones, Benjamin, Rexfield, Born: Nov. 6, 1876 in Virginia, Parents Not Given
Jones, Susie Anna, Rexfield, Born: Nov. 22, 1897 in Virginia, Father: Arthur Carpenter, Mother: Mildred Hollens
Miller, James Thomas, Rexfield, Born: Feb. 11, 1870 in Virginia, Father: James Miller, Mother: Ellen Meadows
Miller, Lela Rose, Rexfield, Born: March 25, 1895 in North Carolina, Father: Wm. Michael, Mother: Cordelia Weston
Robinson, Nelson, Rexfield, Born: March 10, 1867 in Virginia, Parents Not Given
See, John, Rt. 3 Lovilia, Born: Aug. 4, 1884 in Schuyler Co., Missouri, Father: Joseph See, Mother: Not Given
Stovall, Warren Henry, Rexfield, Born: Nov. 17, 1910 in Hiteman, Iowa, Father: Andrew Stovall, Mother: Maude Edwards
Smith, Carley, Rexfield, Born: March 1870 in Virginia, Father: William Smith, Mother: Ada Smith
Smith, Lizzie, Rexfield, Born: Feb. 12, 1880 in Virginia, Father: Robert Howard, Mother: Elvira Jackson
See, Charles, Rexfield, Born: Jan. 25, 1879 in Tennessee, Father: Jerry See, Mother: Delia See
See, Betty, Rexfield, Born: 1891 in Kentucky, Parents Not Given
Thompson, Richard, Lovilia, Born: Sept. 18, 1900 in Mississippi, Father: Richard Thompson, Mother: Elizabeth Rise
Toran, Edward, Rexfield, Born: Aug. 3, 1885 in North Carolina, Father: Not Given, Mother: Annie Malone
Toran, Mary, Rexfield, Born: April 22, 1887 in Munchakinock, Iowa, Father: James Bates, Mother: Mary Sims
Williams, Fannie, Lovilia, Born: Nov. 25, 1875 in Missouri, Father: Ephriam Mickers, Mother: Mary Stephens
Woodford, Hester, Rexfield, Born: Dec. 8, 1880 in Harrisburg, Pennsylvania, Father: Marshall Brock, Mother: Margaret Wood
Ward, Walter, Rexfield, Born: July 11, 1877 in Oklahoma, Father: Henry Ward, Mother: Not Given
Bryson, John, Lovilia, Born; March 12, 1890 in Virginia, Father: Fred Bryson, Mother; Rosa Howard
Bryson, Charity, Lovilia, Born: April 30, 1900 in Alabama, Father: Scott Colly, Mother: Ida Bell
Estes, Leonard, Lovilia, Born: Aug. 1886 in Missouri, Father: Henry Estes, Mother: Mary L. Blue
Estes, Lizzie, Lovilia, Born: Sept. 1868 in Virginia, Father: Jackson Winton, Mother: Letta Howe
Nance, W.M., Lovilia, Born: June 12, 1874 in Virginia, Father: Dr. Nance, Mother: Leams Martin
Nance, Amanda, Lovilia, Born: June 27, 1874 in Virginia, Father: Sam Rodgers, Mother: Rachel Bailey
Rumley, Carl, Lovilia, Born: Aug. 30, 1910 in Monroe Co., Iowa, Father: General Rumley, Mother: Pearl Warner

Wayne Township:
Boles, Henry, Melrose, Born: Jan. 12, 1894 in Iowa, Father: Henry Boles, Mother: Alice Watkins
Boles, Minnie, Melrose, Born: Sept. 2, 1887 in Missouri, Father: Oscal Tonsil, Mother: Isabelle Berry
Brooks, Wirte B., Melrose, Born: Aug. 20, 1877 in Missouri, Father: Flemming Brooks, Mother: Lizzie Roocher
Brooks, Mattie, Melrose, Born: Feb. 16, 1870 in Missouri, Father: James Rutherford, Mother: Catherine Ray
Bell, Myrtle M., Melrose, Born: Feb. 23, 1895 in Missouri, Father: W.B. Brooks, Mother: Mattie Rutherford
Garnett, William, Melrose, Born: July 15, 1858 in Virginia, Father: Churchill Garnett, Mother: Ann Pitts
Garnett, Vica, Melrose, Born: May 2, 1867 in Missouri, Father: John Robinson, Mother: Kora Crouty
Hill, Homer, Melrose, Born: March 15, 1863 in Alabama, Father: Thomas Hill, Mother: Rebecca Erwin
Hogsette, Bessie, Melrose, Born: Sept. 27, 1891 in Iowa, Father: Jess Jones, Mother: Lucy Unnamed
Harris, Harry, Melrose, Born: Sept. 1885 in Virginia, Father: Alf Harris, Mother: Elizabeth Unnamed

LeeAnn Dickey

Jackson, Robert, Melrose, Born: March 14, 1856 in Virginia, Father: Robert Jackson, Mother: Margaret Merchant
Johnson, Hattie, Melrose, Born: April 10, 1885 in Alabama, Father: Henry Head, Mother: Malissa Walker
Lobbins, Emanuel, Melrose, Born: Sept. 2, 1877 in Missouri, Father: Matt Lobbins, Mother: Sarah Mathews
Miller, James, Melrose, Born: Dec. 31, 1910 in Monroe Co., Iowa, Father: Josh Miller, Mother: Hattie Head
Morrison, George Jr., Melrose, Born: March 14, 1897 in Missouri, Father: George Morrison, Mother: Hattie Trewaters
Morrison, George Sr., Melrose, Born: July 19, 1867 in Missouri, Father: William M. Morrison, Mother: Bell Hughs
Nolan, Lewis, Melrose, Born: Nov. 6, 1882 in Iowa, Father: Lewis Nolan, Mother: Julia Robinson
Rogers, Ed, Melrose, Born: 1857 in North Carolina, Father: Sam Rogers, Mother: Rachel Bailey
Tate, Albert, Melrose, Born: March 28, 1882 in North Carolina, Father: Sidney Tate, Mother: Roxanna Unnamed
Tate, Logan, Melrose, Born: April 9, 1881 in North Carolina, Father: Ike Tate, Mother: Laura McNelia
Tate, Millard, Melrose, Born: Sept. 23, 1885 in North Carolina, Father: Sidney Tate, Mother: Roxanna Unnamed
Tobin, John, Melrose, Born: Sept. 18, 1907 in Iowa, Father: James Tobin, Mother: Mattie Higgins
Turner, Enoch, Melrose, Born: July 29, 1891 in Alabama, Father: Charles Turner, Mother: Mary Unnamed
Ward, John, Melrose, Born: Sept. 8, 1854 in Georgia, Father: John Ward, Mother: Susan Unnamed
Waites, Dan, Melrose, Born: Nov. 12, 1868 in Virginia, Father: Wm. Waites, Mother: Carrie Brown
White, James C., Melrose, Born: May 10, 1852 in Kentucky, Father: James White, Mother: Jane Garnett
Yancy, George D., Melrose, Born: Feb. 9, 1871 in Virginia, Father: Madison Yancy, Mother: Lucy Boles

Buxton Memorial, located in a roadside park in Lovilia, Iowa, not far from the site of Buxton. (Michael W. Lemberger)

Buxton in 1968

In 1968, photographer Michael Lemberger visited Buxton along with former resident Dutch Jones and documented what remained of the town.

Right: Vault from company office.
Below: Dutch Jones in front of the warehouse for the company store (see page 136).
Far right: Jones looks at the foundation of the company store.
Right, below: Reservoir dam at center left with remaining buildings.

© Michael W. Lemberger

Buxton Today

Efforts are underway to clear brush from the site and to add signs marking the remaining structures.

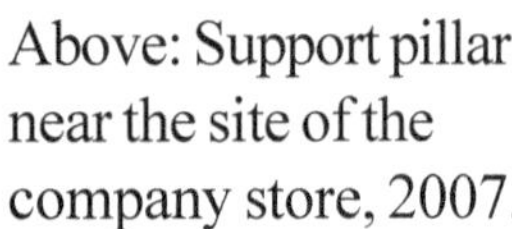

Above: Support pillar near the site of the company store, 2007.

Above right: The remains of a Buxton street, 2007.

Right: Warehouse for the company store, 2007. (see page 134.)

(Photos by Michael W. Lemberger)

About the Authors

LeeAnn Dickey is a dedicated genealogist who started researching her own family tree and ended up seeking out records and documentation for families across the nation. She is also a proud mother and grandmother. She lives in Albia, Iowa. Her email address is dickeyleeann@yahoo.com.

LeAnn Lemberger is better known to readers as novelist Leigh Michaels, the author of more than 80 novels and non-fiction books. More than 30 million copies of her books are in print. Her website is www.leighmichaels.com.

Michael W. Lemberger is an artist, photographer and historian. After more than 50 years as a professional photographer, he has arranged to donate his collection of photographic images to the University of Iowa Libraries. His website is www.mlemberger.com.

About the Publisher

PBL Limited is a commercial publisher of niche-market fiction. For more information about books, authors, or submission requirements, please visit www.pbllimited.com. Some of our titles are pictured on the next page.

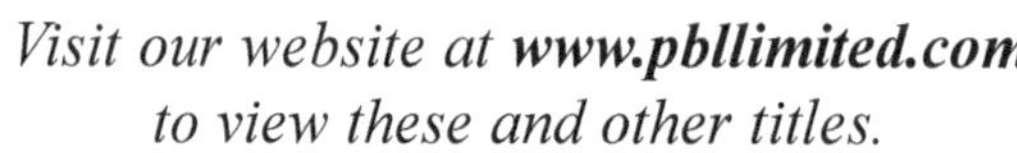

Iowa's Proud Heritage — Loren N. Horton

www.ingramcontent.com/pod-product-compliance
Lightning Source LLC
LaVergne TN
LVHW080921110826
845155LV00039B/109

* 9 7 8 1 8 9 2 6 8 9 7 2 6 *